TOTAL GUITAR

WORKOUT

Practice Skills

EXERCISES FOR SPEED, STRENGTH & STAMINA

LUKE ZECCHIN

Getting lost on the guitar neck?
Finally, fretboard memorization made easy!

If you like this book, you'll love our *Fretboard Memorization Workshop*! This online master class is your shortcut to demystifying the fretboard puzzle. Here you'll be guided step-by-step through the key concepts, techniques, and exercises needed to master your entire fretboard—quickly and easily. These insights have helped thousands of students worldwide, and we're certain they'll help you too!

For more information, head to **LearnYourFretboard.com**.

This book is dedicated to my brother, Aaron. Sorry I skipped recorder and went straight to guitar—it worked out.

Published by **GuitarIQ.com**

Copyedited by Allister Thompson

Proofread by Dan Foster

Illustrated by Jasmin Zecchin

The author and publisher have made every effort to ensure the information contained in this book is both relevant and accurate at the time of release. They accept no responsibility for any loss, injury, or inconvenience sustained by any person using this book or the information provided within it.

Please Note: This guide was written to help improve your guitar playing technique. It isn't intended as a substitute for any form of medical diagnosis, treatment, or therapy. The information provided in this handbook in no way constitutes professional medical advice. If you experience consistent pain or regular discomfort when playing guitar, please seek the advice of a qualified medical professional who can assist you personally with this issue.

Contents

Get Your Free Online Bonus Now!

This book comes complete with free online bonus material. We've compiled a companion website to enhance your reading experience. Extras include audio examples, backing tracks, bonus downloads, and more!

Get your free bonus content at: **www.guitariq.com/tgw-bonus**

Preface

Welcome, and thank you for choosing *Total Guitar Workout*.

So, why a workout book for guitar? After all, we learn guitar to play music, not exercises! Admittedly, this is a (not entirely unwarranted) criticism of many exercise books. Effective practice requires a healthy balance. It should explore new ideas, engage with things creatively, and never be reduced to a string of disconnected technical drills with no system or agenda.

That said, it would be foolish to dismiss the notion of exercises altogether. Just because something isn't the complete picture doesn't mean it's not a crucial part of the puzzle. Would you play an entire basketball game just to practice your free throws, or a complete tennis match just to work on your serve? Of course not! It would only waste time and distract you from those specific skills needing attention.

Ultimately, playing music is the culmination of many parts working together. The better we can isolate and develop these individual mechanics, the better our performance as a whole. Used properly, practice drills are the best tool available for enhancing and refining the core elements of our guitar playing.

To that end, this book explores step-by-step the key mechanics for building stamina, coordination, dexterity, and speed. These exercises are bite-sized, simple to learn, and easy to incorporate into practice sessions of any length. They can be adapted into quick warm-ups, expanded into intense workouts, and even used to inspire new creative ideas. All this from the comfort of your couch!

I sincerely hope this book will help you discover your untapped potential and breach new levels of axe-wielding wizardry!

—Luke Zecchin

Introduction

Great performance is a byproduct of great practice. A well-rounded routine might involve warm-ups, skill development, learning songs, writing music, and experimenting with new ideas (not to mention a healthy dose of jamming!). While exercises shouldn't dominate your entire practice, they're a vital part of it.

The question is: Where do you start? (Let alone what to do next and how to know what works.) Finding things to try isn't the issue; the guitar world is filled with a myriad of warm-ups and exercises. The problem is organizing and making sense of it all. An abundance of random, disjointed practice drills will likely produce more confusion than anything useful.

Total Guitar Workout is the product of equal parts passion and necessity. Here you'll discover a complete, start-to-finish workout system for guitar. This book was carefully designed to drill down on the most important mechanics for the widest impact on your playing. It provides enough structure for clear guidance and direction but enough flexibility for experimentation and creativity. In short, this is your step-by-step, jam-packed, no-nonsense guide for achieving results!

How does it work? This book is organized into eight chapters. The sections within each chapter are designed to flow methodically through the numerous topics covered. As such, it's generally recommended (but not necessary) to work through the book in order. Doing so will provide the broadest scope, allowing you to revisit your favorite sections later. You can then customize your own workouts around the exercises you find particularly useful or relevant.

As a basic overview, the workouts in this book are described in four parts. These outline the *how*, *what*, *why*, and *where* of each exercise. They're explained as follows:

- **How to Do It:** Provides an overview and playing example for each exercise.
- **What to Focus On:** Highlights the three main focus points to keep in mind.
- **Why It's Beneficial:** Briefly explains the reason behind each practice drill.
- **Where to Next:** Outlines the next steps for maximizing each workout.

All that said, how you use this book is ultimately up to you; it isn't meant to be prescriptive. If you'd like to start with specific chapters first, skip or repeat certain sections, or even explore your own tangents entirely...then let your enthusiasm guide you! This book exists to inspire and point you in the right direction. While it's responsible for the teaching, you're responsible for the learning—so have fun with it!

Finally a small word of caution The following exercises range from seemingly simple to deceptively difficult and beyond. Therefore, it's important to be mindful of your body and move at your own pace. As always, common sense is king. Start slowly, be conscious of playing fatigue, take regular breaks, and if something hurts, stop. (Don't be a hero!) We're all different, so trust your intuition and learn on your own terms. Who knows, your *inner* teacher just might surprise you.

The Ground Rules

Ready for the guitar domination to begin? Great! Before getting started, it's important to establish some basic ground rules. These essentials will help you stay on track and get the most benefit from each exercise. They're outlined as follows:

- **Prime the Pump:** You wouldn't work out your body without warming up. Why treat your hands any differently? Gentle stretching, light massage, and circular movement through your joints are great ways to get the blood flowing. As a guitar player, the fingers, hands, and wrists are your greatest assets—look after them!

- **Start Slowly:** Anyone can play almost anything if they do it slow enough. Using the percussion tracks provided, begin each exercise at a comfortable tempo. Be sure to focus on accuracy; learning isn't a race! What's the point in playing something badly at a fast tempo? Sloppy practice only yields sloppy playing.

- **Work Easy:** Always remember, *how* you do something is just as important as *what* you do. Unnecessary tension, excessive force, and exaggerated motion are common ways we make ourselves work harder than necessary. Keep it light. Learn to minimize and refine your movements. Your technique will thank you!

- **Customize It:** Make sure each workout works for you. When asking things like, *How long should I practice*? *How many repetitions should I do*? or *When should I move forward, go back, or take a break*? the answer is always: Let your body guide you. If it's working, keep going; if it's not, tweak things until it does!

- **Gauge Your Progress:** Once comfortable with an exercise, challenge yourself! You won't grow if you don't test the edges of your ability. Increase your tempo in small increments, using the percussion tracks provided to track your progress. Improving your skills means constantly pushing those goalposts forward!

- **Monitor Your Mindset:** Good practice involves training your mind, not just your fingers. At its core, practice is simply problem-solving. It's about identifying issues and finding solutions. Being overly judgmental or critical of yourself is unhelpful! A healthy level of emotional detachment from the process does wonders for that inner critic.

- **Practice Smarter:** The frequency of your practice is more important than the time spent practicing. If you have limited time (and who doesn't!), try balancing this evenly over the week. For example, 20-30 minutes of quality practice every day is significantly more beneficial than a 3 to 4-hour practice binge over the weekend!

- **Think "Big Picture":** The reasoning behind each exercise is more important than the exercise itself. Once you understand the concepts and why they're beneficial, the specifics can be adapted in all sorts of ways. Try to think *beyond* the exercises themselves and always consider things in light of real playing situations.

- **Explore and Experiment:** Practice drills are completely malleable. They can be moved, altered, reversed, and totally mashed together. For example, you might try one position across all six strings. What about trying all positions across one string? Why not switch fingers, shapes, and even guitars, if it helps? Don't be afraid to get creative!

- **Keep It Musical:** The goal of technique is to serve musicality. Ask yourself, *Could this exercise be translated to different chord shapes or scale patterns?* And if so, *How could it be turned into a new lick, riff, or song idea?* Maintaining this perspective will help you engage more meaningfully with each workout.

1

Right-Hand Percussion

To kick off, let's fortify our foundations! This chapter examines the cornerstone of great playing: solid right-hand technique.

Overview

Most technique-based exercises for guitar focus on the arena of the left hand. After all, it's the one that takes center stage. It's the acrobat, agile and graceful, dancing around the fretboard with speed and finesse (well, at least that's the goal!). The truth is, however, that without a rhythmically solid right hand, the left hand is destined to flounder and trip over itself.

While right-hand technique is sometimes the forgotten sibling when talking about speed and dexterity, it's equally important. This book could hardly be called **Total Guitar Workout** if we neglected such an important fact. As such, these first two chapters are dedicated solely to developing great picking technique.

The following workouts are exercises in right-hand *percussion*. Working with the right hand in isolation means we can be intentional with our focus. When we're not distracted by the left hand, it allows us to better pinpoint weak spots and concentrate on problem areas. So, let's put those tasty blues chops on hold for a minute—it's time to think like a drummer! (Now that's a phrase you'll seldom hear me say.)

The (Not So) Basics

Almost every scale or arpeggio pattern on guitar uses one of three basic variations: *one* note per string, *two* notes per string, or *three* notes per string. In this first section, we'll look at the mechanics of these movements in detail. To do this, we'll isolate the right hand and experiment with some basic rhythmic patterns across all six strings. While these exercises are simple, executing them cleanly can be surprisingly difficult!

Exercise 1.1

How to Do It

Starting with your left hand in the middle of the guitar neck, rest your fingers gently over the strings to ensure that they're muted. With your guitar pick, slowly play through all six strings (up and back) using alternating down/up strokes. Here's an example of this exercise using quarter notes (one note per beat):

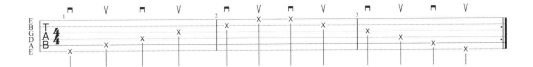

What to Focus On

- Be sure to keep all six strings muted; you shouldn't hear any notes ringing.
- Concentrate on keeping your timing consistent (it helps to tap your foot).
- Make sure you alternate evenly between strokes, focusing on accuracy.

Why It's Beneficial

Alternate strokes are the foundation of good picking technique. One-stroke-per-string exercises sound easy, but they can be unexpectedly difficult. Isolating your right hand allows you to concentrate solely on your timing and picking accuracy.

Where to Next

Once comfortable, repeat this exercise, starting with an *upstroke* (instead of a downstroke). Your picking strokes will now alternate in the opposite direction; be sure to maintain this *up/down* motion throughout the entire exercise. As we move through this section, this simple shift is fantastic for highlighting those pesky weak spots in your technique.

How to Do It

This next exercise is similar to the previous one. However, this time we'll add *two* strokes per string and play 8th notes (two notes per beat). Again, mute the guitar strings with your left hand and practice looping through all six strings, using alternate strokes. Here's a demonstration:

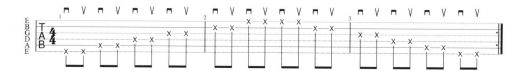

What to Focus On

- Concentrate on keeping strokes consistent when switching between strings.
- Keep relaxed to avoid excess tension in your hand, wrist, forearm, and elbow.
- Try lightly resting your right palm on the guitar bridge for added stability.

Why It's Beneficial

Guitar players regularly use two-note-per-string picking patterns (with pentatonic scales, for example). Looking at this mechanic in isolation allows you to better develop your picking speed and fluency.

Where to Next

As with the previous exercise, try starting with an upstroke instead of a downstroke. Having switched your picking strokes in the opposite direction, be sure to maintain this sequence throughout the exercise.

Exercise 1.3

How to Do It

This is another right-hand isolation exercise. However, this time we'll use *three* strokes per string and play triplets (three notes per beat). As before, mute the strings with your left hand, looping through alternate strokes across all six strings. For example:

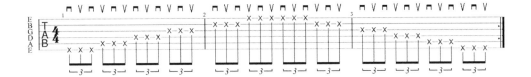

What to Focus On

- Practice accenting the first stroke of every triplet to help maintain your timing.
- Focus on accuracy to reduce accidental contact between the pick and strings.
- Minimize your picking action to avoid excessive or exaggerated movements.

Why It's Beneficial

Three-note-per-string picking patterns are common in guitar playing (with modal scales, for example). As with the previous exercises, isolating your picking technique allows you to better concentrate on any problem areas.

Where to Next

Ready for the next challenge? As before, practice alternating your picking strokes in the opposite direction.

Beyond the (Not So) Basics

In this second section, we'll step things up a notch by introducing some additional picking patterns. These include common groupings such as *four* notes per string and *six* notes per string, plus the oddball grouping of *five* notes per string (less common but more interesting!). Like the previous section, not only do these exercises make great practice drills, they also comprise many of the basic mechanics needed in everyday playing.

Exercise 1.4

How to Do It

Rest your left hand over the guitar strings to ensure they stay muted. With your right hand, slowly loop through all six strings, picking four strokes per string. This example uses alternate strokes, playing 16th notes (four notes per beat):

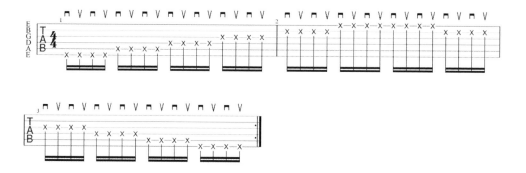

What to Focus On

- For best results, try positioning your pick at a 45° angle to the strings.
- Keep your palm resting lightly on the guitar bridge for added stability.
- Practice accenting the first stroke of each beat to help with your timing.

Why It's Beneficial

For guitar players, 16th-note picking patterns are extremely common (especially in rock music). Breaking down the mechanics of this action is crucial for developing speed and accuracy in your picking technique.

Where to Next

Once comfortable with this exercise, try starting with an upstroke instead of a downstroke. Make sure to alternate your picking strokes consistently throughout the full exercise.

Exercise 1.5

How to Do It

Building on the previous exercise, this time let's add *five* strokes per string (again playing 16th notes). As before, practice looping through all six muted strings using alternate strokes. Don't get confused by the change in time signature, just count in groups of five as follows:

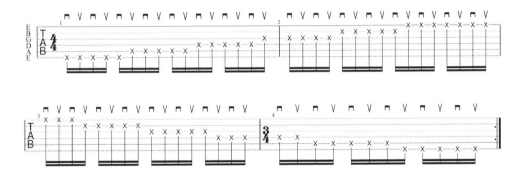

What to Focus On

- To start with, it helps to sound out a five-syllable word, such as "e-lec-tri-ci-ty."
- Despite the added difficulty, try to maintain a consistent beat with your foot.
- Focus on keeping your picking strokes clean and consistent between strings.

Why It's Beneficial

Admittedly, five-note-per-string picking patterns are less common in guitar playing. (Fusion players may disagree!) However, they're fantastic for stretching both your brain and your picking ability.

Where to Next

Just to make things a little more challenging…again, let's vary this exercise, starting with an upstroke. As before, be sure to alternate your picking strokes consistently. For an extreme challenge, try playing *quintuplets* (five-notes-per-beat) instead of 16th notes—but don't call me if your brain explodes!

How to Do It

As one final rhythmic variation to this exercise, let's add *six* strokes per string, this time playing 16th-note triplets (six notes per beat). Again, practice looping through all six muted strings using alternate strokes. For example:

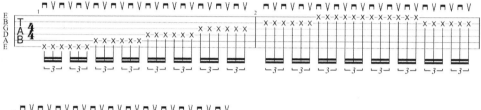

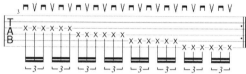

What to Focus On

- As a general rule, hold your pick securely with no more than a third showing.
- When increasing speed, remember to stay relaxed to minimize excess tension.
- Avoid lifting your guitar pick higher than necessary when crossing strings.

Why It's Beneficial

Despite being the largest rhythmic grouping we've looked at, six-note-per-string patterns are quite popular in guitar playing (especially for speed picking). As with the previous exercises, examining your picking technique in isolation is fantastic for maximizing right-hand fluency.

Where to Next

Yep, you guessed it! Extend this exercise by alternating your picking strokes in the opposite direction.

Skipping the (Not So) Basics

This final section on right-hand percussion will test even the best and brightest. Here we'll spice up the previous exercises by isolating different string combinations –from simple to extreme! Navigating between different string sets is one of the more challenging right-hand tasks. Mastering this may require some time in the woodshed. Just remember, you can't reach higher without stretching yourself first!

Exercise 1.7

How to Do It

This first exercise is about adding movement to the percussive ideas from the previous sections. To do this, we'll introduce a basic *three-steps-forward, one-step-back* pattern. Be sure to practice this with all the rhythmic variations we've covered, from quarter notes (one stroke per beat) to 16th-note triplets (six strokes per beat). This example uses triplets:

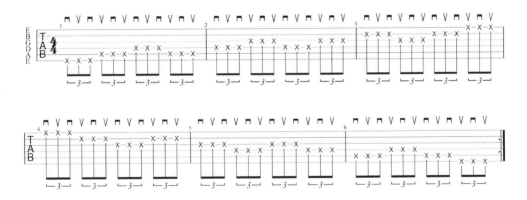

What to Focus On

- As before, remember to keep the open strings muted with your left hand.
- Again, this is an exercise in *alternate* picking; keep your strokes consistent.
- Start slowly to maintain clean and comfortable strokes before speeding up.

Why It's Beneficial

This section focuses on taking your picking chops to the next level! Adding movement to the previous exercises helps you develop a more robust picking technique.

Where to Next

Starting with an upstroke, vary this exercise by switching your picking strokes in the opposite direction. You should have the hang of this by now!

Exercise 1.8

How to Do It

Next, let's add a basic *string-skipping* sequence to our right-hand exercises. This pattern simply leapfrogs one string before taking a step back. Again, practice this with all the different rhythmic variations we've looked at. For this example, we'll use 16th notes:

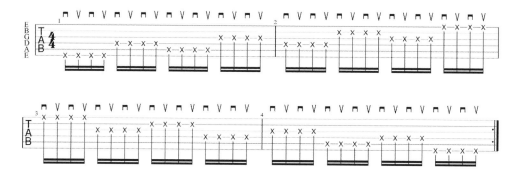

What to Focus On

- Minimize your alternate strokes. (Imagine your pick is stuck to the strings.)
- Focus on accuracy, remembering to use the guitar bridge for extra stability.
- Despite the difficulty of string skipping, avoid excessive picking movements.

Why It's Beneficial

Once you're able to move freely between adjacent strings, string skipping is the next hurdle. (Pardon the pun!) Not only is this great picking practice, learning to skip strings fluently is also key for breaking familiar patterns and injecting more interest into your playing.

Where to Next

You know the drill: Now try all variations of this exercise by alternating your picking strokes in the opposite direction.

How to Do It

Finally, let's conclude this chapter on right-hand percussion with arguably the mother of all picking exercises. This exercise takes string skipping to the extreme! To do this, remain on the low E string and practice alternating between every string combination. (Remember, try this with each rhythmic variation we've covered.) This example uses triplets:

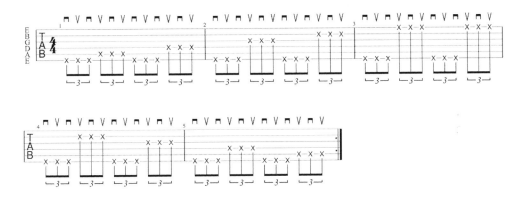

What to Focus On

- To begin with, practice looping between just two strings at a time.
- Despite the larger string distances, make sure your timing remains solid.
- Keep your pick close to the strings, remember, you're skipping–not *leaping*.

Why It's Beneficial

This is the ultimate exercise in alternate picking accuracy! Of course, guitar players rarely need to skip more than one or two strings when playing. However, being able to execute bigger skips makes smaller ones feel effortless in comparison.

Where to Next

Starting with an upstroke, practice alternating your picking in the opposite direction. (I bet you didn't see that coming!) For those wanting extra credit, try flipping the entire exercise around, skipping back and forth from the high E string.

2

Right-Hand Precision

Having covered the rudiments, here we'll explore the role of dynamics in developing a more expressive picking technique.

Overview

If we reduce guitar technique to its bare bones, what is it? Simple: The left hand controls *what* notes are played; the right hand controls *when* notes are played. Right? Well, in essence, yes. However, this definition overlooks one crucial feature of playing music: *how* notes are played.

For example, imagine a world where people communicated only by SHOUTING! We might use the right words. We might even use them in the right context. However, we'd be neglecting one of the most important aspects of communication. How we say something is often more important than the actual words used. (It's marriage counseling 101, folks!)

As beginners, picking dynamics are often the first thing we overlook. After all, it's hard enough getting the left hand to behave, let alone consider the nuances of what our right hand is doing! However, this doesn't mean right-hand dynamics aren't important. It means they're part of what moves a beginner past the point of *sounding* like a beginner. Developing right-hand control is one of the most important tools you have for improving your tone. (It's also much cheaper than buying pedals!)

Attack Those Notes

The tone produced by your picking hand is a mix of multiple variables (e.g., the angle of your pick to the strings, the type of pick being used, the placement of your hand, etc.). However, you could argue that the basic technique itself isn't so nuanced. In general terms, the picking hand has two options: playing sustained (or *legato*) notes or playing stabbed (or *staccato*) notes. In this section, we'll take a detailed look at these two types of pick attack.

Exercise 2.1

How to Do It

For this first exercise, let's begin on the open G string. At a comfortable tempo, practice playing quarter notes (one note per beat), 8th notes (two notes per beat), triplets (three notes per beat), 16th notes (four notes per beat), and 16th-note triplets (six notes per beat) in a looped sequence. Keep your alternate strokes even and let each note sustain for its full duration. For example:

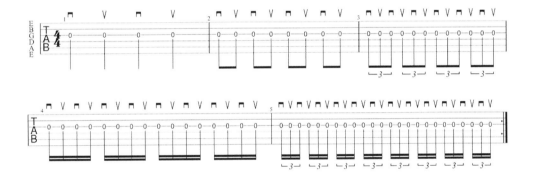

What to Focus On

- Again, this is an isolated picking exercise. Give that left hand a coffee break!
- Concentrate on keeping your strokes consistent in both volume and timing.
- Ensure that notes sound clearly but avoid exaggerating your picking motion.

Why It's Beneficial

This basic exercise helps with picking consistency and developing right-hand stamina. It also lays our foundation for the following sections.

Where to Next

When comfortable with this exercise, experiment by increasing the tempo in small increments. Make sure you practice this drill across all six strings.

Exercise 2.2

How to Do It

Next, let's repeat the previous exercise with one important variation. Instead of letting notes ring out, this time cut each note short, using *only* the guitar pick. To do this, strike the string with one side of the pick and then immediately stop it with the other. When done properly, this should produce a short, stabbed-sounding staccato note. Here's the outline:

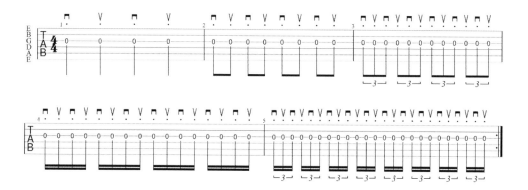

What to Focus On

- Ensure notes sound clearly, while keeping each stroke as short as possible.
- This is entirely a right-hand action—your left hand shouldn't touch the string.
- The goal is to make this staccato technique feel like one fluid movement.

Why It's Beneficial

While this might sound easy, it can be a difficult technique to master. It's a fantastic exercise for picking control and learning to minimize your right-hand movements. (Tip: This idea of *economizing* your technique is crucial for building speed and stamina.)

Where to Next

As before, once you're able to do this cleanly, experiment with more challenging tempos using all six strings.

How to Do It

For this final variation, let's practice alternating between *both* sustained and stabbed notes. Do this by making every downstroke a sustained note and every upstroke a stabbed note. To better contrast your pick attack, we'll limit the exercise to quarter notes, 8th notes, and triplets, as shown:

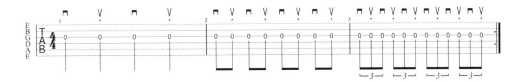

What to Focus On

- After each upstroke, rest the pick on the string before the next downstroke.
- Remember to hold your pick securely, placing it at a 45° angle to the strings.
- For increased accuracy, try using a tapered pick that's 0.73mm (or thicker).

Why It's Beneficial

Basic variations in pick attack are often overlooked when first learning guitar. Exploring the sound and feel of contrasting strokes adds greater expression and dynamics to your playing.

Where to Next

As with the previous exercises, once comfortable, experiment with higher tempos across all six strings.

Express Those Notes

Having looked at pick attack, let's consider a few other key variables. Your picking hand is responsible for more than hitting the right notes at the right time. It also controls the overall dynamic of your playing. There are three important factors to keep in mind: the *pressure* used to play notes, the *placement* of your pick, and the *position* of your hand. These fundamentals directly impact the volume, tonality, and character of each note you play.

Exercise 2.4

How to Do It

This exercise builds on the previous section. We'll again isolate the open G string and move through different rhythmic variations (from quarter notes to 16th-note triplets). However, this time let's focus on the *dynamic range* of your picking. Instead of sounding notes consistently, loop the exercise by varying your pick intensity. To do this, move between loud and quiet notes as follows:

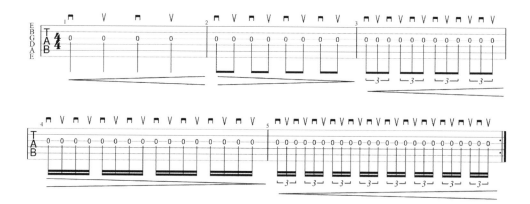

What to Focus On

- As before, this is a right-hand exercise—keep that left hand benched for now!
- Be sure to emphasize the full range of your strokes, from quietest to loudest.
- Try keeping your pick close to the string at all times, even for louder notes.

Why It's Beneficial

Learning what to play is only half the equation; the other part is learning *how* to play. Picking dynamics are one of the simplest (and most powerful) tools we have for injecting feeling and emotion into our playing.

Where to Next

Try this exercise using *stabbed* notes instead of sustained notes (see the previous section, if needed). Be sure to practice this drill across all six strings.

Exercise 2.5

How to Do It

Having looked at dynamics in volume, the next step is experimenting with changes in tonality. To do this, loop the previous exercise, this time shifting the position of your pick along the string. Moving toward the guitar neck, the sound becomes warmer and fuller. Moving toward the bridge, the tone chimes with a more nasal quality. Practice varying the placement of your pick to explore these different tonalities.

(Please refer to the audio example.)

What to Focus On

- Move slowly between the bridge and neck positions, sounding notes clearly.
- Compare the sound and feel of each stroke between these two extremes.
- Rest your pinky and ring fingers on the guitar body for added support.

Why It's Beneficial

Great tone isn't about the brand of guitar you use—it's about your hands! And it starts with the basics of how each note is played. While we all love an excuse to buy more gear, investing in your technique is the most essential (and least expensive) thing you can do to improve your sound.

Where to Next

Again, repeat this exercise using stabbed notes. Make sure you practice this drill on all six strings.

Exercise 2.6

How to Do It

Having looked at variations in volume and tone, let's consider the timbre, or quality, of our notes. Just like the piano, your guitar comes with a dampening pedal—it's attached to your right hand! To begin, rest the fleshy part of your palm where the string meets the bridge. Moving your hand along the string, notes become increasingly muted or choked-sounding. Repeat the previous exercise, this time experimenting with the placement of your palm, instead of your pick.

(Please refer to the audio example.)

What to Focus On

- Explore the varying levels of palm muting produced by your right hand.
- Focus on alternating smoothly between sustained and muted notes.
- Keep your hand, wrist, and elbow relaxed in order to move freely.

Why It's Beneficial

Besides picking (and strumming), dampening is the most important function of your right hand. It's essential for muting strings not being played and altering the tonal character of your notes.

Where to Next

Like the previous exercises, experiment with stabbed notes and repeat this drill using all six strings.

Control Those Notes

Now that we're familiar with the fundamentals of great right-hand technique, let's conclude by applying these ideas in a more musical context. To do this, we'll introduce some basic chord shapes into the mix. (You heard me, tell that left hand to warm up–time to get in the game!) Remember, don't be fooled by the seeming simplicity of these exercises. The better you get, the more important the fundamentals become.

Exercise 2.7

How to Do It

In this exercise, we'll take the first two notes in a major chord and practice moving between them. The purpose is to experiment with right-hand dynamics in a more harmonic context. Staying on the D and G strings, practice looping your pick attack from loud to soft. This example starts from the 7th fret, using 8th notes:

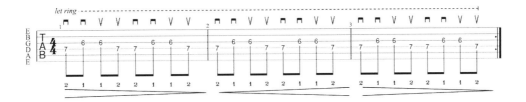

What to Focus On

- Unlike the previous sections, this exercise is limited to using 8th notes.
- Focus on your timing, shifting smoothly between loud and soft notes.
- Note that this exercise no longer adheres to strict alternate picking.

Why It's Beneficial

Besides developing your picking dynamics across multiple strings, this drill is a basic introduction to *sweep* picking. In contrast to alternate picking, this technique links multiple strokes moving in the same direction. (Another fantastic method for injecting speed and fluidity into your playing!)

Where to Next

Repeat this exercise, experimenting with the other dynamic variations from the previous section. (For example, the tonal differences created by the placement of your pick and different levels of right-hand dampening.)

Exercise 2.8

How to Do It

Next, let's take the previous exercise but include all three notes from the major chord. Using triplets, practice sweeping between the D, G, and B strings by shifting your pick attack from loud to soft. Here's the exercise starting from the 7th fret:

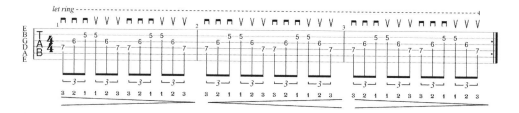

What to Focus On

- Note that, besides adding the 5th, this exercise replaces 8th notes with triplets.
- Dynamics should be controlled by your pick—keep that left hand planted.
- Avoid exaggerating your picking motion when shifting to louder notes.

Why It's Beneficial

Like the previous two chapters, this exercise maintains an intense focus on right-hand technique. As mundane as isolated picking exercises might seem, mastering these fundamentals will improve every aspect of your playing!

Where to Next

Repeat this exercise, experimenting with other dynamic variations like pick placement and right-hand dampening.

How to Do It

For this final variation, let's add the 7th to our major chord, creating four notes in succession. Playing 16th notes, practice sweeping across the D, G, B, and E strings—again, alternating between loud and soft strokes. For example:

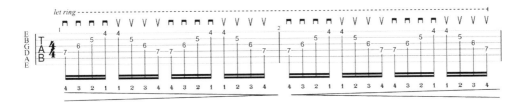

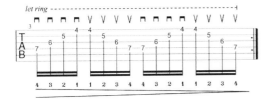

What to Focus On

- This exercise now uses all four fingers and requires that you play 16th notes.
- Remember, hold your pick at a 45° angle to help glide through the strings.
- Try accenting the beat with your guitar pick to maintain better timing.

Why It's Beneficial

Bravo—this is the final isolated right-hand exercise! While sweep picking typically avoids sounding notes together, this technique creates an interesting *arpeggio* effect when played cleanly at faster tempos.

Where to Next

As before, repeat this exercise, experimenting with pick placement and right-hand dampening. If you're feeling brave, try playing all variations of this exercise at half-speed using stabbed notes—I dare you!

3

Left-Hand Finger Gym

In this chapter, we'll shift focus from right-hand drills to examine the fundamentals of left-hand strength and dexterity.

Overview

Congratulations! You've graduated to the next stage in your guitar domination. Your right hand has earned a break (perhaps even a massage and manicure). It's now time to turn our attention to the arena of the left hand. If the right hand is the rhythmic engine of your playing, the left hand is seated in the cockpit. Just like a drummer and lead singer, they need to work together for a band to produce anything vaguely musical (easier said than done, depending on the band!).

As mentioned, the left hand is often seen as the acrobat—the one responsible for towering feats of speed, agility, and finesse. While this interaction between your left hand and the guitar strings can seem complex, at its core it's quite simple. The left hand performs three basic functions. These are *pressing*, *bending*, and *sliding*. Apart from tuning occasionally and twiddling with amp settings, that's basically it!

Although it may seem overly simplistic, these left-hand articulations are at the heart of everything we play on guitar. In this chapter, we'll explore these key mechanics in detail. To do this, we'll isolate the left hand through a series of workouts designed to develop strength, stamina, and control.

Note: On the guitar, fingers are often referred to using names, letters, or numbers. For this book, left-hand fingerings can be referenced as follows:

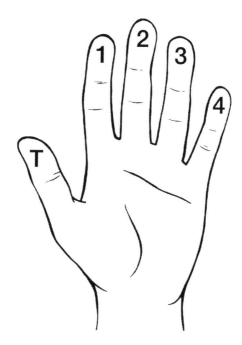

The Big Squeeze

As established, the left hand performs three basic maneuvers on guitar: pressing, bending, and sliding. This section covers the first of these: *pressing*. To state the obvious, guitar notes are created by touching strings to fret wires. Sounding and stopping notes requires both pushing down and lifting up. The following exercises are designed to overemphasize these mechanics by increasing resistance. Much like conventional strength or endurance training, it's easy to run a sprint when you've trained for a marathon!

Exercise 3.1

How to Do It

Without pressing down, rest all four fingers gently on the high E string between the 7th and 10th frets. Starting with your 1st finger, push down firmly and hold for 5-10 seconds. Apply the maximum amount of pressure that's comfortable—but don't hurt yourself, kids! Keep the other three fingers as relaxed as possible, touching the string but *not* pressing down. Repeat this a few times before moving through all four fingers, pressing and holding each finger in sequence.

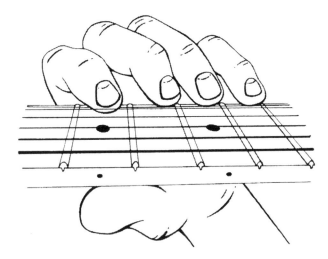

What to Focus On

- This is an isolated left-hand exercise—give that right hand a hard-earned nap!
- Press down firmly but don't overdo it. (If it hurts, you're pressing too hard.)
- Release your hand to shake out any residual tension between repetitions.

Why It's Beneficial

This exercise has multiple benefits. Working your fingers harder than normal builds calluses and finger strength. (And makes normal playing feel significantly easier in comparison.) Learning to apply tension while keeping relaxed (simultaneously, in different parts of the hand) is essential for developing speed and endurance.

Where to Next

Now, try this exercise in various places on the fretboard. Make sure to practice it across all six strings, using all four fingers.

Exercise 3.2

How to Do It

This next exercise is an inversion of the previous one. Instead of placing your fingers above the high E string, this time tuck them *underneath*. All four fingers should sit directly on the fretboard, letting the string rest across your fingernails from above. Start by lifting your 1st finger against the pressure of the string. Hold this for 5-10 seconds, keeping your other fingers relaxed. Repeat this a few times before moving through all four fingers in sequence.

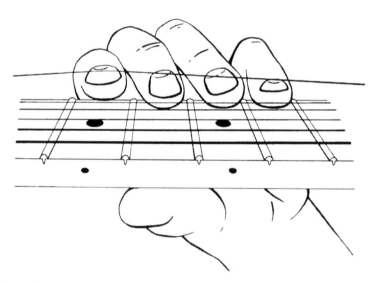

What to Focus On

- Lift each finger only until you feel resistance. Start gently, and if it hurts, stop!
- If the string tension feels uncomfortable, try moving closer to the 12th fret.
- Remember to keep the fingers that aren't in action as relaxed as possible.

Why It's Beneficial

Yep, this exercise is a doozy! We sometimes forget that our fingers *lift* just as much as they press. Working both sides of this motion is great for developing strength and control. Not only is it a good workout, it's great for finger independence too.

Where to Next

Again, try this exercise in multiple places on the fretboard. (Keep in mind, the thicker the strings and the closer your hand to the headstock, the more resistance you'll encounter.)

Exercise 3.3

How to Do It

In this final variation, we'll build on the previous two exercises by using different finger combinations. As with **Exercise 3.1**, start with all four fingers resting above the high E string. Instead of pressing just one finger, this time squeeze your 1st and 2nd fingers down together (leaving the others resting on the string). Repeat the process of holding and releasing, using every finger combination outlined below:

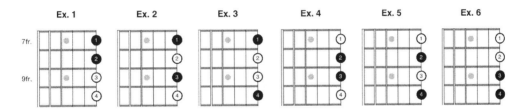

What to Focus On

- Don't go overboard with this! Take a break if your hand gets tired.
- Apply pressure only where it's needed. Why work harder than necessary?
- Remember to breathe normally and shake out any tension between repetitions.

Why It's Beneficial

Controlling tension in multiple fingers at once takes real coordination. (But, hey, as guitar players that's part of the job description!) Again, this is a great workout for developing strength, stamina, and finger independence.

Where to Next

You guessed it...let's take this exercise and invert it! Using the different combinations outlined, now place your fingers underneath the high E string to practice your finger lifts. As before, ensure that you try these exercises in various places on the fretboard, across all six strings.

The Big Bend

Having covered the first function of the left hand, pressing, this section explores the second. *Bending* is like pressing, except that our fingers shift along a different axis. Instead of moving in and out (in proximity to the fretboard), the fingers move up and down (across the face of the fretboard). Admittedly, this task is made much harder by the increased string resistance. As such, the following exercises are targeted workouts for building strength and stamina—definitely not for the faint-hearted!

Exercise 3.4

How to Do It

Start by placing your 1st finger on the 7th fret of the G string. Bend the string down (toward the floor) using the tip of your finger and hold for 5–10 seconds. Keeping your hand relaxed, repeat this action a few times, shaking out any residual tension between repetitions. Next, move through each finger in turn by repeating this exercise on the subsequent three frets.

What to Focus On

- You needn't pick the notes; this is an isolated left-hand strength exercise.
- Bend until you feel an appropriate level of resistance—don't strain yourself!
- Keep your wrist straight and avoid wrapping your thumb over the fretboard.

Why It's Beneficial

Beyond being great for building calluses, this drill focuses on strength and stamina. Bending and vibrato are key parts of guitar vocabulary. (After all, they're something piano players can't do!) Developing the strength necessary across all four fingers is essential for control and accuracy.

Where to Next

Now, practice executing each bend in the opposite direction. Instead of pulling down, bend and hold the string by pushing up (toward the ceiling). Remember to work this drill using all four fingers.

Exercise 3.5

How to Do It

With your 1st finger on the 7th fret of the G string, place your 2nd finger on the 8th fret of the D string. Using both fingers, bend each string in opposite directions from one another (pulling the G string *down* while pushing the D string *up*). Hold this for 5–10 seconds before relaxing and repeating. Next, continue this exercise using the 2nd and 3rd fingers, followed by your 3rd and 4th fingers.

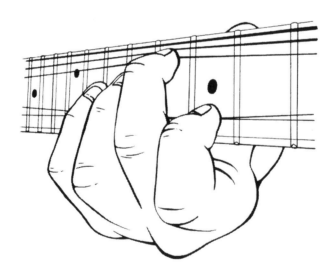

What to Focus On

- Start gently, gradually increasing the level of resistance when comfortable.
- Remember to use the tips of your fingers to maintain their natural curve.
- Avoid squeezing too hard against the guitar neck with your thumb.

Why It's Beneficial

Yeah, this is another tough one, all right! We're literally taking the previous exercise and doubling the intensity. Remember, developing finger strength takes time. Go slowly and don't overdo it!

Where to Next

Now, try swapping each set of fingers around (staying on the same frets but switching strings) to practice bending in the opposite direction. Don't forget, it's important to spend equal time (if not more) working on your weaker finger combinations.

Exercise 3.6

How to Do It

For one final variation, let's repeat the previous exercise using *non-adjacent* fingers. (In other words, your 1st and 3rd, 1st and 4th, and then 2nd and 4th fingers). As before, moving through these different finger combinations, practice bending the G and D strings in opposite directions. Hold each stretch for 5–10 seconds, relax, and repeat.

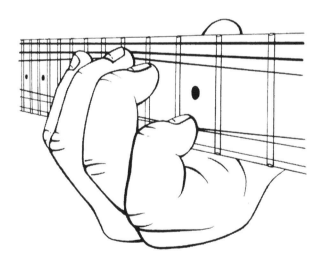

What to Focus On

- Remember, loosen up and breathe normally to avoid any excess tension.
- Again, use your thumb for support, being careful not to squeeze too hard.
- Leave an air gap between your palm and the guitar—don't clamp the neck.

Why It's Beneficial

You thought the previous exercise was tough! Again, this drill is fantastic for developing hand strength and finger independence. Just don't overdo it, macho man (and/or woman, as the case may be).

Where to Next

Switch each finger combination around to practice bending in both directions (again, staying on the same frets but alternating strings). For an added challenge, gradually increase resistance by bending the strings more, holding each stretch for longer, or moving closer to the headstock.

The Big Slide

In this final section, we'll explore the third basic left-hand maneuver: *sliding*. Yet again, here our fingers must navigate along a new axis (albeit a more exaggerated one). If pressing moves in and out (from the fretboard) and bending moves up and down (across the fretboard), then sliding moves back and forth (along the fretboard). This mechanic isn't so much about strength as it is control. Here, we'll outline some key exercises for increasing the precision of this technique.

Exercise 3.7

How to Do It

This exercise is based on the low E string. Start by hammering your 1st finger down on the 3rd fret to produce a clear note (*without* any help from your right hand). Keeping the note sustaining, slide your finger up to the 7th fret. This should sound smooth, like one fluid motion. Next, repeat this action with your other three fingers in sequence (hammering on the 3rd fret and sliding to the 7th). Loop this cycle, moving up and back through all four fingers.

(Please refer to the audio example.)

What to Focus On

- Sound notes using only your left hand. (The right hand's turn will come soon!)
- Try keeping the hammered note consistent in volume across all four fingers.
- Position the pad of each finger to keep the 4th and 5th strings from ringing.

Why It's Beneficial

This drill introduces two key components: hammer-ons and slides. Both techniques are essential in guitar vocabulary. Looping this exercise across all four fingers will highlight any weak spots.

Where to Next

Now, practice this exercise on all six strings. Once you have it under your fingers (literally!), try it in *reverse*, hammering on the 7th fret and sliding down to the 3rd.

How to Do It

Next, we'll extend the previous exercise. The core concept is the same, except the interval being used is larger (a fifth instead of a major third). Starting on the low E string with your 1st finger, practice hammering on the 3rd fret and sliding to the 10th. Again, cycle this sequence, looping through all four fingers.

(Please refer to the audio example.)

What to Focus On

- As before, keep each note consistent in volume across all four fingers.
- Don't tense your hand. Squeezing too hard will impede your movement.
- Position your thumb comfortably in (or slightly above) the middle of the neck.

Why It's Beneficial

This drill requires both strength and control. Executing slides accurately becomes increasingly harder with larger intervals.

Where to Next

Again, try this exercise across all six strings. Once comfortable, practice it in reverse, starting from the 10th fret.

Exercise 3.9

How to Do It

For this final exercise, let's extend our range to span an entire octave! Starting with your 1st finger, cycle through all four fingers by hammering on the 3rd fret and sliding up to the 15th. As before, loop this action, moving through each finger in sequence.

(Please refer to the audio example.)

What to Focus On

- Look for your target note, taking care not to fall short or overshoot.
- Keep your slides smooth. The individual notes shouldn't be discernible.
- Practice increasing the speed of each slide to really test out your accuracy!

Why It's Beneficial

Slides on guitar usually fall within one octave. Learning to move fluently between these extremes (with all four fingers) makes smaller intervals a piece of cake by comparison.

Where to Next

You know the drill! Practice this exercise on all strings before trying it in reverse, starting from the 15th fret.

4

Left-Hand Finger Yoga

Moving from power to finesse, we'll continue our left-hand workouts with targeted exercises in finger independence and coordination.

Overview

Bravo! You've reached the final chapter on isolated hand exercises. Did you imagine getting this far into the book having barely used both hands together? Well, this book is different than most! It's not about learning songs, licks, or playing tricks; it's about something more important. Breaking down, isolating, and working on the smallest playing mechanics that will yield the biggest improvements. Remember, the bigger picture is always the sum of individual brush strokes.

If the previous chapter resembled a series of gym-like finger drills, this chapter takes a very different tack. These exercises are less like gym workouts and more like yoga classes. Of course, the goal remains the same: developing left-hand dexterity and control. That said, now we'll switch gears from building strength and stamina to mastering independence and coordination.

In this chapter, we'll explore a series of workouts focused not on power but on *precision*. These will range from the seemingly simple to the frustratingly difficult. (Keep in mind, aiming higher might involve smashing a few ceilings.) So, grab your guitar, a cup of coffee, a sprinkling of patience, and let's get started!

The Big Bounce

The previous chapter looked at overemphasizing the various mechanics of the left hand to build strength and stamina. In contrast, this chapter focuses on keeping your movements as *understated* as possible. Power and endurance are important, but good technique also requires finesse and subtlety. In this first section, we'll explore a series of drills designed to test your finger independence.

Exercise 4.1

How to Do It

Starting from the 7th fret of the A string, place your remaining fingers diagonally (as outlined below). With all four fingers planted down, begin gently pressing and releasing your 1st finger. Loop this action to create a slow, bouncing motion. (Ensure that your finger stays in contact with the string–the movement should be subtle.) Continue this exercise with your three remaining fingers, working each finger in turn.

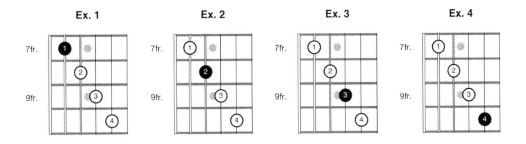

What to Focus On

- Again, this exercise isolates the left-hand–good to do while watching TV.
- When pressing and releasing, avoid lifting your finger off the string.
- Ensure that your static three fingers remain held down at all times.

Why It's Beneficial

This is a fantastic exercise for finger independence. The name of the game is small, controlled movements. (Essentially, that's all guitar playing is! A series of little actions coordinated to express something musical.)

ı comfortable, try inverting the diagonal shape of your fingers. To do
ıe your 4th finger on the 10th fret of the A string, staggering your remaining
ıgers the opposite way.

Exercise 4.2

How to Do It

Using the diagonal shape from the previous exercise, let's take the idea of small, controlled movements and add another layer of difficulty. This time, instead of bouncing your fingers in isolation, practice pressing and releasing each finger once in succession. Do this by looping up and back, lifting and planting your fingers in sequence, as follows: 1-2-3-4-4-3-2-1.

(Refer to the previous diagram if needed.)

What to Focus On

- As before, keep your fingers in contact with the strings at all times.
- Make sure that each finger not in use remains planted down.
- Loop slowly through all four fingers and avoid pressing too hard.

Why It's Beneficial

This is another little gem for developing finger independence! Like much of this book, the simplest workouts can be unexpectedly difficult.

Where to Next

As with the previous exercise, repeat this left-hand drill by inverting the diagonal shape of your fingers.

Exercise 4.3

How to Do It

This final variation moves things up a notch. (You wouldn't want me to go easy now!) Using the same diagonal shape as before, we'll practice pressing and releasing fingers in succession. This time, however, let's introduce some basic string skipping into the mix. To do this, loop up and back, gently lifting and pressing each finger in the following order: 1-3-2-4-4-2-3-1.

(Refer to the initial diagram in **Exercise 4.1**, if needed.)

What to Focus On

- Remember, this exercise is all about developing control—it isn't about speed!
- Again, keep movements minimal and don't lift your fingers from the strings.
- Avoid gripping the fretboard, and maintain the natural curve of your fingers.

Why It's Beneficial

Getting your fingers to behave can be hard work! (If it were easy, we'd all be virtuosos.) While these exercises are fantastic for finger independence and control, they also reinforce the idea of economic movement—a central theme in masterful playing.

Where to Next

Again, extend this workout by inverting the diagonal shape of your fingers.

Really Big Bounce

Keeping with the diagonal shape from the previous section, it's time to step things up a little! Unlike the first few exercises, this section focuses on coordinating multiple fingers in unison. To do this, we'll start by pairing the fingers next to one another before exploring non-adjacent finger sequences. Again, the focus is on precision and control. So much about good technique hinges on these two principles.

Exercise 4.4

How to Do It

With your 1st finger on the 7th fret of the A string, space your remaining fingers diagonally (as outlined below). With all four fingers planted, gently release your 1st and 2nd fingers before pressing them down again. Slowly loop this bouncing motion with both fingers in coordination. Next, complete this exercise, working your 2nd and 3rd fingers, followed by the 3rd and 4th fingers in turn.

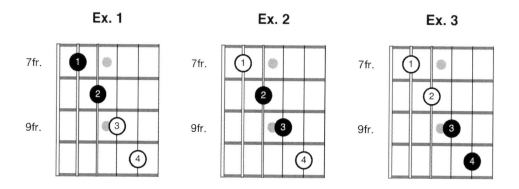

What to Focus On

- Remember, the bouncing motion shouldn't lift your fingers off the strings.
- Make sure you coordinate both fingers to press and release in unison.
- Keep your other two fingers held down without pressing too hard.

Why It's Beneficial

Like the previous section, this is a fantastic finger independence workout. Learning to bounce multiple fingers while leaving others planted is sure to test your coordination (and likely your patience!).

Where to Next

Now, repeat this exercise by inverting the diagonal shape of your fingers. Do this by placing your 4th finger on the 10th fret of the A string and stacking your remaining fingers accordingly.

Exercise 4.5

How to Do It

Sticking with our trusty diagonal shape, let's experiment with *non-adjacent* fingers. Beginning with all four digits pressed down, gently release your 1st and 3rd fingers. As before, loop this bouncing motion with both fingers in coordination. Next, complete the workout by switching to your 2nd and 4th fingers.

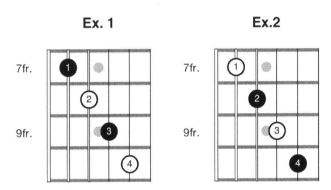

Ex. 1   **Ex.2**

What to Focus On

- Keep both fingers moving together, pressing and releasing in unison.
- Remember, your other fingers should remain in place without moving.
- Don't squeeze too hard. Be mindful of any excess tension in your hand.

Why It's Beneficial

Yep, things just got a little harder! If the previous exercise didn't test that steely patience of yours, this one certainly will.

Where to Next

Again, extend this exercise by inverting the diagonal shape of your fingers.

How to Do It

Now that you're getting the hang of it, let's cycle through some different sequences. Using our diagonal shape, practice looping between each set of adjacent fingers. Do this by bouncing your 1st and 2nd, 2nd and 3rd, and then 3rd and 4th fingers in succession. Once comfortable, change this sequence to alternate back and forth between both sets of non-adjacent fingers.

(Refer to the two previous diagrams if needed.)

What to Focus On

- Again, concentrate on moving each set of fingers in unison—it's not easy!
- Remember, move in sequence, bouncing each pair of fingers only once.
- Stay relaxed and avoid raising your thumb too high over the fretboard.

Why It's Beneficial

Okay, don't panic! If this exercise is difficult, rest assured…it's meant to be. This kind of serious control takes time to develop. Go slowly and don't get too frustrated with your fingers. (They're only little, after all.)

Where to Next

We're not quite done yet. Be sure to repeat this exercise, inverting the diagonal shape of your fingers.

The Really Big Switch

Finally, the silent assassin of isolated left-hand exercises! Like the previous section, we'll continue testing our coordination and independence using multiple sets of fingers. However, instead of bouncing fingers in place, these exercises involve swapping strings. This added level of difficulty is fantastic for whipping that mischievous left hand into obedience. Go gently with this one, but make sure to persist—you'll thank me later.

Exercise 4.7

How to Do It

Like the previous sections, we'll begin with our basic diagonal shape. But this time, instead of bouncing different fingers in place, let's focus on switching them around. To start with, practice alternating strings with your 1st and 2nd fingers, leaving the others in place. (Note: You're only switching strings, not frets.) Loop this action before moving to your 2nd and 3rd, and then 3rd and 4th fingers, as illustrated:

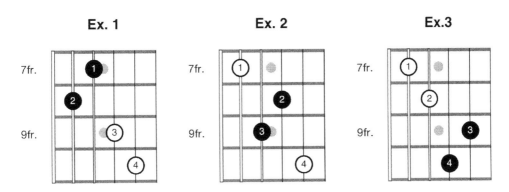

What to Focus On

- Again, this is an isolated left-hand exercise. (The chords sound ugly anyway!)
- Focus on coordinating both fingers to alternate positions at the same time.
- Control your movements to avoid exaggerating the shift between strings.

Why It's Beneficial

Yep, this is another little gold mine for honing your finger independence and control. (Might as well put that TV time to good use!)

Where to Next

As with the previous exercises, extend the challenge by inverting the diagonal starting position of your fingers.

Exercise 4.8

How to Do It

Starting again from our base shape, let's expand on the previous exercise by working the *non-adjacent* fingers. To begin, practice alternating strings with your 1st and 3rd fingers (leaving the other two in place). Once this movement feels controlled, switch to alternating your 2nd and 4th fingers as follows:

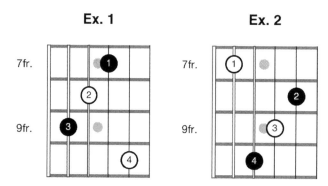

What to Focus On

- Pay attention to landing accurately on your fingertips when shifting strings.
- Remember to keep both static fingers planted securely without moving.
- Relax your thumb, leaving a gap between your palm and the fretboard.

Why It's Beneficial

How's that patience going? Yep, this one's even harder than the last. Sorry. Well, I did promise a workout—it's in the title!

Where to Next

What's that? You want another challenge! Try flipping this exercise to invert your diagonal starting position.

How to Do It

Okay, time to raise the bar! For this final variation, let's switch between multiple sets of fingers in *succession*. To do this, alternate your 1st and 2nd, 2nd and 3rd, and then 3rd and 4th fingers in series. Practice looping through each variation (returning to the starting position in between). Next, continue this exercise using your non-adjacent fingers, alternating the 1st and 3rd and then 2nd and 4th fingers in sequence.

(Refer to the two previous diagrams if needed.)

What to Focus On

- Practice this exercise slowly, concentrating on control and accuracy.
- Focus on transitioning smoothly between the different sets of fingers.
- Be sure to shake out any residual tension if your hand starts tightening.

Why It's Beneficial

Finally, we've arrived at the granddaddy of finger independence exercises! Make sure you stick with this one. It will take time, but it's worth it.

Where to Next

Wait. Did you forget something? Remember to practice this, flipping your diagonal starting position.

5

Fretboard Brainteasers

Ready for the next step? Here we'll embark on a series of challenges to engage the brain and get those hands working together.

Overview

Okay, tell that right hand to suit up—it's time to get back in the game! And speaking of games, that's the subject of this chapter. What better way to get your hands firing than through a series of what we'll call *fretboard brainteasers*? Consider this a strange mix of left-hand Tai Chi and mental Sudoku for guitar players.

The focus here is twofold. First, these exercises are designed to develop coordination. The goal is getting your brain synchronized with both hands—and your hands synchronized with each other. Second, the emphasis will be on *economy of motion*. In other words, training your fingers to stay put by reprogramming their natural tendency to flap about wildly. (A continued theme in this book.)

To do this, we'll start with a twist on an old favorite. It's become a staple for guitar teachers everywhere: the basic four-finger chromatic exercise (sounds exhilarating, right?). From there, however, prepare to kick things into overdrive with a series of tweaks and challenges sure to get those brain juices flowing. Let the games begin!

The Old Faithful

In this section, we'll begin with the most popular (and arguably least exciting) finger exercise in the world. This warm-up may not stretch the borders of your mental or physical capabilities. However, it serves as a good launch pad. With some simple tweaks, we can transform an otherwise mundane exercise into something that's significantly more useful and challenging.

Exercise 5.1

How to Do It

This first drill is a twist on the basic four-finger exercise we all know and love (or loathe!). Start on the 5th fret of the low E string and ascend using all four fingers. Moving between the 5th and 8th frets, cycle this pattern across each string as demonstrated. Sound familiar? Well, there's a catch! You must keep each finger held down for as long as possible, lifting *only* when required on the adjacent string.

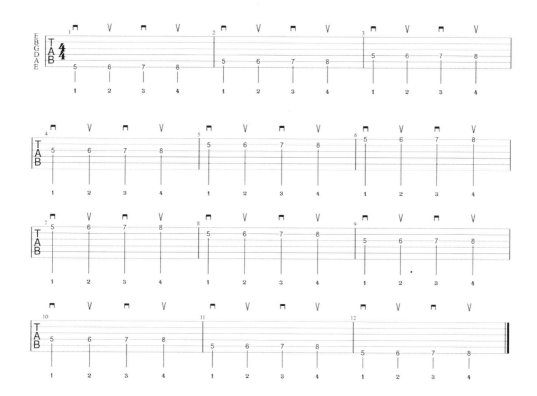

What to Focus On

- It's very important not to rush this exercise. Go slowly and focus on accuracy.
- Keep both hands synchronized by picking and fretting in one unified motion.
- Once a note is played, don't lift that finger until it's needed on the next string.

Why It's Beneficial

This is another unexpectedly challenging exercise. Again, the emphasis here is on *control*—teaching those fingers to stay put instead of just waving about! It's a great workout for finger independence and economizing your movement.

Where to Next

Try this exercise in reverse (starting on the 5th fret of the high E string). Practice beginning with an upstroke to invert your picking action.

Exercise 5.2

How to Do It

For this next exercise, we'll add to the challenge by experimenting with different starting points. Beginning the pattern from each finger creates four distinct sequences. These are: 1-2-3-4, 2-3-4-1, 3-4-1-2, and 4-1-2-3. Moving between the 5th and 8th frets, practice all four variations across each string. To demonstrate, this example starts with the 2nd finger on the 6th fret:

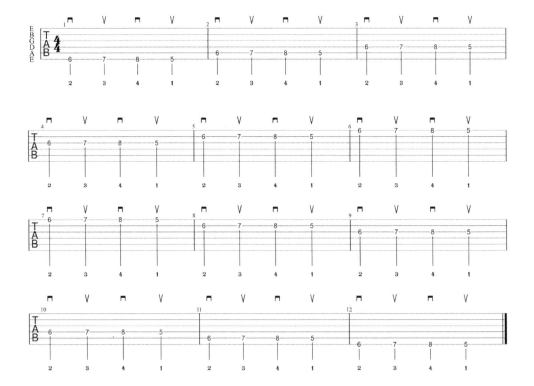

What to Focus On

- Again, keep your fingers planted after each note, only lifting them as necessary.
- Go slowly, being careful to apply the minimum required left-hand pressure.
- Make sure you can play each sequence cleanly before moving to the next.

Why It's Beneficial

This challenges your brain and fingers to approach the same thing from a different perspective. As such, it adds a bit more spice to an otherwise pedestrian exercise.

Where to Next

Now, practice each variation in reverse, beginning on the high E string with an upstroke.

Exercise 5.3

How to Do It

Like the previous exercise, this final variation moves through each sequence starting from different frets. However, for a little more color, we'll also skip the second note in each pattern (before completing the sequence). As before, this creates four new variations: 1-3-4-2, 2-4-1-3, 3-1-2-4, and 4-2-3-1. Make sure to practice them all. This example starts with the 1st finger on the 5th fret:

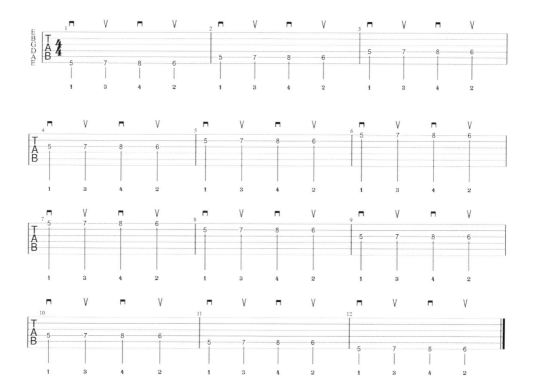

What to Focus On

- Again, start slowly, focus on accuracy, and avoid the temptation of rushing.
- Note that these patterns don't allow your fingers to stay planted for long.
- As such, simply remain in close proximity to the strings where possible.

Why It's Beneficial

Once again, we're injecting a new element of challenge into this exercise. The more we escape the linear 1-2-3-4 sequence, the more it tests our coordination and finger independence (not to mention our mental computing power!).

Where to Next

Reverse each variation of this exercise, starting with an upstroke. If you're feeling adventurous, try skipping every third or fourth note in sequence instead of every second note.

The Old Unfaithful

While the previous section provided some handy warm-ups, here's where things get interesting! Continuing with these chromatic exercises, we can inject more interest into the mix by adding a sprinkling of chaos. (Ready to get that brain working overtime?) Intentionally *short-circuiting* the patterns our fingers are used to forces our brain to re-engage with the task at hand. In short, no sleeping on the job today!

Exercise 5.4

How to Do It

This drill takes the basic pattern from **Exercise 5.1** and flips it on its head. (Warning: Things are about to get weird!) Staying between the 5th and 8th frets, we can create some unique sequences by introducing finger *displacement*. To do this, loop the original exercise, but instead of planting the 1st finger in its usual position, shift it to the adjacent string (leaving the others in place). For example:

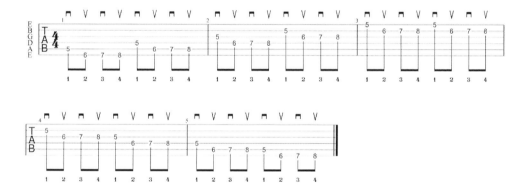

What to Focus On

- Remember, we're just shifting the 1st finger. The 1-2-3-4 pattern is the same.
- Again, practice leaving each finger planted until required for the next note.
- Use alternate strokes and pay careful attention to crossing strings cleanly.

Why It's Beneficial

By placing our basic four-fret pattern across two strings, we completely short-circuit the original sequence. It's very difficult to do this on autopilot—a great drill for engaging your fingers and brain!

Where to Next

Now, repeat this exercise by displacing the other three fingers in turn. (For example, shifting the 2nd finger instead of the 1st, and so on.) Do this one finger at a time, leaving the other three in position. Ensure that you can play each variation accurately before trying the next.

Exercise 5.5

How to Do It

Ready to take things up a notch? Let's repeat the same exercise but alternate our starting point. Using the four patterns beginning from each finger, practice displacing your 1st finger to the adjacent string. (Confused? Basically, take the sequences from **Exercise 5.2**, plus the displacement idea from the previous exercise, and splice them together!) To demonstrate, here's an example using the 3-4-1-2 sequence:

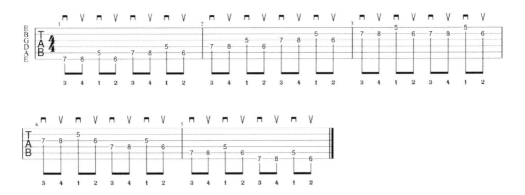

What to Focus On

- You'll notice that some sequences feel more familiar than others—lucky you!
- Leave your fingers planted where possible and avoid exaggerated movements.
- Make sure you can play each pattern cleanly before moving to the next.

Why It's Beneficial

This one will get those mental cogs ticking! It's also a great lesson in creativity. Injecting the familiar with a dose of the *unfamiliar* is an excellent technique for inspiring new and interesting possibilities.

Where to Next

As before, practice this exercise by displacing all four fingers in turn. Remember, we're just taking the four patterns from **Exercise 5.2** (1-2-3-4, 2-3-4-1, 3-4-1-2, 4-1-2-3) and displacing one finger at a time. If you're paying attention, that's 16 different variations in total—better get started!

Exercise 5.6

How to Do It

Next, let's continue messing with the exercises from the previous section, using finger displacement. To do this, we'll begin with the four patterns outlined in **Exercise 5.3**. As before, practice mixing things up by shifting your 1st finger to the adjacent string. Here's an example based on the 2-4-1-3 pattern:

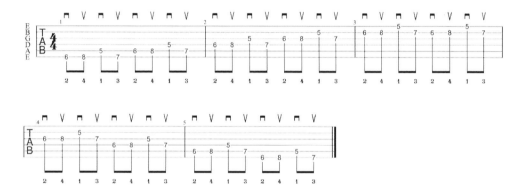

What to Focus On

- Loop this exercise at a tempo that accommodates accuracy—don't rush!
- Remember to stay relaxed, don't press too hard, and breathe normally.
- As always, complete each pattern cleanly before attempting the next.

Why It's Beneficial

Yep, there's a lot to work through in this section—that's kind of the point! This chapter is a workout for your brain, not just your fingers.

Where to Next

You guessed it. Continue this exercise by displacing your other three fingers in turn. Again, we're working with four different patterns (1-3-4-2, 2-4-1-3, 3-1-2-4, 4-2-3-1) and four different fingers. That's another 16 variations in total. Better give that brain a short vacation after this!

The Super Old Unfaithful

Hopefully, you made it through the previous section relatively unscathed. Things are about to get a lot more challenging! Besides infusing our original patterns with finger displacement, here we'll add yet another level of difficulty. This presents an even greater obstacle for your fingers and brain. As such, it's a fantastic workout in control and coordination. Don't panic; you've got this!

Exercise 5.7

How to Do It

Much like **Exercise 5.4**, this drill takes the four-finger pattern we started with and adds finger displacement. The difference is, here we'll displace *two* fingers—not just one! Once again, begin at the 5th fret using the basic 1-2-3-4 sequence. This time, however, practice shifting your 1st and 3rd fingers to the adjacent string (leaving the other two in position). For example:

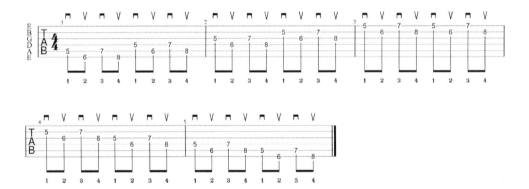

What to Focus On

- Remember, we're just shifting two fingers. The 1-2-3-4 sequence is the same.
- As before, use alternate strokes and focus on crossing strings accurately.
- Keep each finger planted until it's required to move to the next note.

Why It's Beneficial

Building on the previous section, we're again short-circuiting the familiar 1-2-3-4 sequence. The added complexity of shifting strings and applying different finger combinations provides a fantastic all-around workout.

Where to Next

Repeat this exercise by displacing your remaining two fingers. In other words, shift the 2nd and 4th fingers, leaving your 1st and 3rd in position. Ensure that you can loop both patterns cleanly before continuing.

Exercise 5.8

How to Do It

Okay, prepared to test yourself? Good! For this next exercise, we'll use the four sequences starting from each finger (outlined in **Exercise 5.2**). However, as with the previous exercise, let's confuse these patterns by displacing both the 1st and 3rd fingers to the adjacent string. Here's an example starting with the 2-3-4-1 pattern:

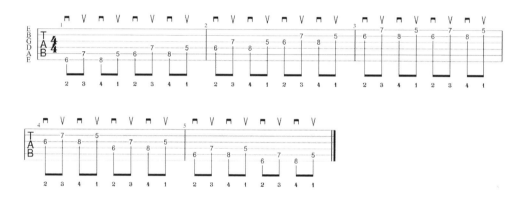

What to Focus On

- Move at a comfortable tempo, making sure to practice each pattern cleanly.
- Remember to focus on control and avoid exaggerating your movements.
- Keep your fingers planted where possible. (It's okay if strings ring together.)

Why It's Beneficial

Confused? Fear not! Once you understand the general concept, the patterns are relatively easy to work out. Of course, the hard part is getting your brain and fingers to cooperate—but again, that's the point.

Where to Next

Now, repeat this exercise by displacing your opposite two fingers (again, shifting the 2nd and 4th fingers out of position, instead of your 1st and 3rd). Remember to practice this using all four sequences!

How to Do It

This final variation isn't for the faint-hearted. (Please resist the urge to throw this book at the TV!) Here, we'll revise the somewhat randomized patterns from **Exercise 5.3**. Once again, looping through each variation, practice shifting your 1st and 3rd fingers out of position. To demonstrate, this example uses the 1-3-4-2 sequence:

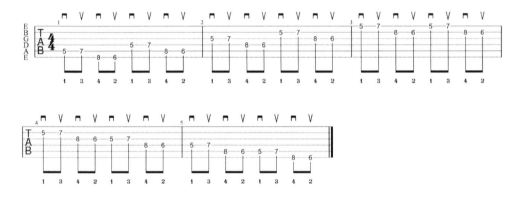

What to Focus On

- For reference, it may be helpful to revisit **Exercise 5.3** and **Exercise 5.6**.
- Don't rush—concentrate on accuracy and economizing your movements.
- Despite the increased difficulty, ensure that your hands remain synchronized.

Why It's Beneficial

Wow, what an epic chapter of mind-bending fretboard madness. Kudos on making it this far! Despite our relatively straightforward starting point, each exercise has required increased patience and mental perseverance—two key attributes in mastering anything!

Where to Next

Again, continue this exercise by displacing your 2nd and 4th fingers. (I might suggest also displacing your 1st and 2nd, and then 3rd and 4th fingers in turn. However, to avoid brains exploding, let's save that for the thrill seekers out there!) Go ahead, reward yourself with some chocolate—you've earned it.

6

Fretboard Finger-Twisters

Continuing our total guitar domination, it's time for an all-out attack with skill-builders designed for speed and fluency.

Overview

If the previous chapter was a combination of Tai Chi and Sudoku for guitar, this chapter could be considered something akin to left-hand *Pilates*. As such, the focus here is on building core hand strength. In contrast to the strength exercises in Chapter 3, here we'll explore a series of workouts inspired by the chromatic ideas from the previous exercises.

To do this, we'll introduce the concept of *legato*, a key technique in guitar playing (especially for those blazing-fast, fret-burning, face-melting rock licks we all love!). From improving the tone and sustain of your notes to increasing playing speed and fluency, there's a gold mine of benefits to uncover here.

The first section starts off with some introductory skill-building ideas. We'll then progress to the main workouts for this chapter before concluding with an explosion of left-hand acrobatics sure to get those fingers working overtime. Rested and well fed? Good. Grab that shirt and tie—it's time for work!

The First Steps

In this section, we'll start with some legato basics. This technique lets you play notes without your right hand, using *hammer-ons* and *pull-offs* (hammering or plucking strings with the fingers of the left hand). This section is essentially a series of warm-ups and skill builders to prepare you for the more advanced workouts in this chapter. Let's get cracking!

Exercise 6.1

How to Do It

For this first exercise, let's start with the absolute basics. Begin with your 1st finger on the 7th fret of the high E string. Pick this note and practice hammering the tip of your 2nd finger down on the next fret. The goal is to produce a clear note equal in volume to the first. Once this sounds even, practice hammering on your 3rd and then 4th fingers in turn, using their respective frets.

(Please refer to the audio example.)

What to Focus On

- Ensure that the volume stays consistent between picked and hammered notes.
- Focus on accuracy, letting each hammered note sustain for its full duration.
- Landing on your fingertips with precision is essential for clean legato notes.

Why It's Beneficial

Seem simple? Even experienced players need to revisit the fundamentals. Use this exercise to concentrate on the attack, sustain, and quality of notes produced by your left hand. These elements are key for smooth, free-flowing legato playing.

Where to Next

Reverse this exercise, starting with the 4th finger on the 10th fret and *descending* to the 3rd, 2nd, and 1st fingers in turn. (Note: When moving to lower frets, we substitute hammer-ons for pull-offs.) To do this, pick the first note and sound the next by plucking the string in a downward motion. Ensure that you practice both variations of this exercise across all six strings.

How to Do It

This next drill is a simple but *extremely* effective legato exercise. Begin with your 1st finger on the 7th fret of the high E string. Practice cycling between frets using hammer-ons and pull-offs to produce a trill-like effect. Start with your 1st and 2nd, then 1st and 3rd, and finally 1st and 4th fingers in turn. Concentrate on two fingers at a time, looping each repetition for as long as is comfortable.

(Please refer to the audio example.)

What to Focus On

- Use *only* hammer-ons and pull-offs (except for the initial note that's picked).
- Focus on consistency in the volume and timing of each note in your trills.
- Start slowly, incrementally increasing the speed and length of your trills.

Why It's Beneficial

Trills combine the two mechanics of legato playing (hammer-ons and pull-offs) in rapid succession. As such, they're excellent for building finger strength and endurance. (Another handy exercise while watching TV!)

Where to Next

Once comfortable, flip this exercise, starting from the 10th fret with your 4th finger, alternating between the pinky and each finger in turn. Be sure to practice both variations of this exercise across all strings.

Exercise 6.3

How to Do It

Building on the previous exercise, let's extend each trill to incorporate all four fingers. Starting on the 7th fret of the high E string, this time practice looping back and forth between each finger in *succession* (alternating your 1st and 2nd, 1st and 3rd, and 1st and 4th fingers, in sequence). For example:

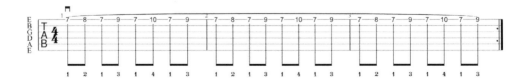

What to Focus On

- Look to maintain consistency in the volume and timing of each note.
- Monitor your hand tension and apply no more pressure than necessary.
- Try to restrict other strings from ringing using the palm of your right hand.

Why It's Beneficial

Again, here the focus is building strength and endurance. The added challenge of alternating between all four fingers will also test your accuracy and coordination. (Gotta be cruel to be kind!)

Where to Next

As before, switch this exercise, starting with your 4th finger and moving in reverse. Make sure you practice both variations on all six strings. (Work that pinky, baby!)

The Next Steps

Now that we've worked on the fundamentals, let's step things up! This is where **Chapter 6** earns the title *"Fretboard Finger-Twisters."* In this section, we'll infuse the chromatic patterns from the previous chapter with our newfound love of legato. Expanding your legato playing across multiple strings requires strength, accuracy, and coordination. These exercises are some of the best weapons in your arsenal for left-hand domination. Time to hit the front line, soldier!

Exercise 6.4

How to Do It

For this first exercise, we'll start easy. Here's a simple twist on the original four-finger drill outlined in **Exercise 5.1**. Starting on the 7th fret of the low E string, use hammer-ons to ascend chromatically with all four fingers. Cycle this pattern across each string (picking only *once* per string) as shown:

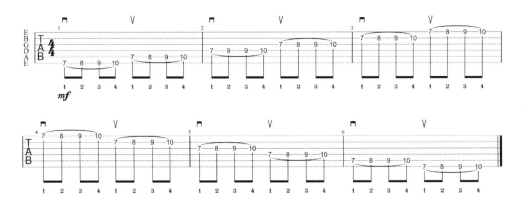

What to Focus On

- Ensure that each note sustains cleanly. (Think of a piano hammering its strings.)
- Start slowly, focus on timing, and keep every note consistent in volume.
- Be mindful of tension buildup in your hand—if it hurts, take a break!

Why It's Beneficial

This exercise expands the technique from the previous section, linking it across multiple strings. Legato is often used to play fluid-sounding runs in this way. (The word *legato* literally means being "tied together" in a smooth/flowing manner.)

Where to Next

Starting from the 10th fret of the high E string, reverse this sequence across all six strings using pull-offs.

Exercise 6.5

How to Do It

In this exercise, we'll continue looking at patterns from **Chapter 5** with a renewed focus on legato. Alternating our starting point, let's revisit the four sequences outlined in **Exercise 5.2** (1-2-3-4, 2-3-4-1, 3-4-1-2, 4-1-2-3). Practice looping all four sequences using legato, picking only *once* per string. This example outlines the 3-4-1-2 pattern:

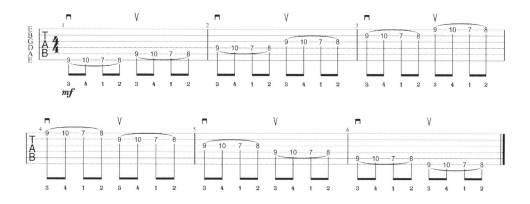

What to Focus On

- Note that these sequences now require *both* hammer-ons and pull-offs.
- Along with your palm, try using your 1st finger to help mute open strings.
- Make sure you play each sequence accurately before moving on to the next.

Why It's Beneficial

This is where we step things up! Combining hammer-ons and pull-offs can feel tricky at first. Start slowly and be sure to persist. Trust me, your hands will thank you later!

Where to Next

Now, try repeating all four sequences *without* picking any notes! To do this, hammer on the first note of each string instead of using a pick. (Tip: It's helpful to mute the open strings with your right hand. Do this by reaching across your body and gripping just below your guitar's headstock. A great trick for super-clean legato runs!)

How to Do It

Finally, let's revisit the sequences outlined in **Exercise 5.3**. Here we started from different frets, skipping the second note in each pattern (1-3-4-2, 2-4-1-3, 3-1-2-4, 4-2-3-1). As in the previous section, practice looping all four sequences, picking once per string, and using legato. To demonstrate, here's an example using the 4-2-3-1 variation:

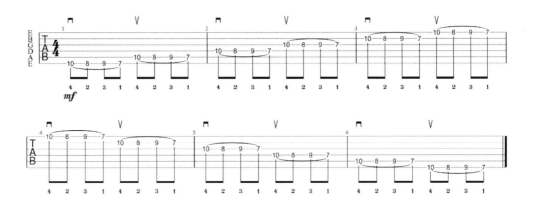

What to Focus On

- Once again, these sequences require both hammer-ons and pull-offs.
- Remember, the harder the pattern, the greater the need for accuracy.
- As always, be sure to play each sequence cleanly before moving on.

Why It's Beneficial

Feel like things are getting harder? You're right! Executing these sequences requires strength, accuracy, dexterity, and coordination—all the reasons you bought this book! That's why legato is such a great practice tool.

Where to Next

As before, try playing all four sequences without your guitar pick. Do this by hammering on the first note of each string. Again, experiment with positioning your right hand across your body to mute the open strings.

Forget the Steps

The previous section used the metaphor of adding *weapons* to your arsenal. Sticking with this theme, let's launch a grenade into the mix! (A splash of mayhem never hurt anybody, right?) In this section, we'll use our chromatic patterns to experiment with various string sequences. This technique is very popular, especially in legato playing. Another one that's sure to test your strength, accuracy, coordination, and (did I mention)...*patience*?

Exercise 6.7

How to Do It

To start with, let's ease in by using everybody's favorite four-finger chromatic exercise. This first sequence adds some repetition into the mix by echoing the four notes after every upstroke. Be sure to try this using both hammer-ons (ascending from the 7th fret) and pull-offs (descending from the 10th fret). To demonstrate, this example uses hammer-ons:

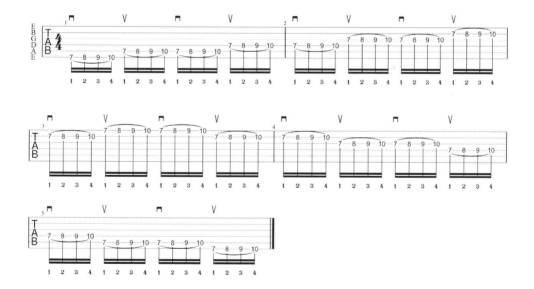

What to Focus On

- Remember to keep notes clear and even. (In other words, don't rush!)
- When comfortable, try increasing your tempo in small increments.
- Don't exaggerate your left-hand gestures when sounding notes.

Why It's Beneficial

Applying new string sequences to old patterns is fantastic for getting more mileage from the stuff you already know. Try it out when you're next practicing scales!

Where to Next

Once you have this sequence under your fingers, apply it to the other chromatic patterns we've looked at. Start with the first four variations outlined in **Exercise 5.2** (1-2-3-4, 2-3-4-1, 3-4-1-2, 4-1-2-3). Then move to the other four alternatives from **Exercise 5.3** (1-3-4-2, 2-4-1-3, 3-1-2-4, 4-2-3-1). Sounds like a lot of work? It is! Better get started.

Exercise 6.8

How to Do It

This next sequence moves in a simple *three-steps-forward, one-step-back* motion. As before, let's explore this with the simplest of our chromatic patterns. Moving between the 7th and 10th frets, be sure to practice both hammer-ons and pull-offs. This example outlines the latter:

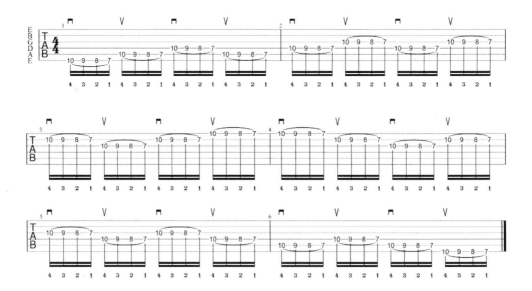

What to Focus On

- As always, start slowly, making sure you can distinguish each note clearly.
- Remember that playing notes cleanly is more about accuracy than force.
- Try positioning both hands to prevent the open strings from ringing.

Why It's Beneficial

String sequences are common in legato/speed playing. Coordinating all four fingers on one string is easy (once you get the hang of it). Transitioning smoothly *between* strings—now that's a challenge!

Where to Next

Experiment with using the eight other chromatic patterns outlined in **Chapter 5**. Feeling adventurous? Again, try muting the open strings with your right hand (positioning it between your left hand and the headstock) and practice each pattern without any picking!

Exercise 6.9

How to Do It

In this final variation, let's ramp things up with a little game of leapfrog! Sticking with our basic chromatic pattern, practice *skipping* every second string as outlined. Again, try this using both hammer-ons and pull-offs. Here's an example illustrating pull-offs:

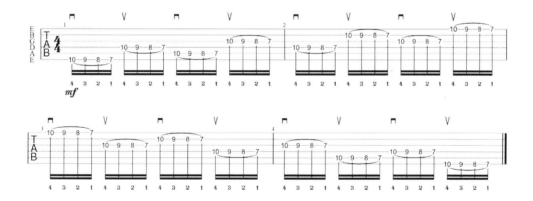

What to Focus On

- Cultivate precision, ensuring that your fingertips land squarely behind each fret.
- Where possible, use your palm and 1st finger to minimize any string noise.
- Don't be a martyr! Watch out for excess tension or pain in your left hand.

Why It's Beneficial

String skipping is fantastic for breaking out of those tired old patterns. It also provides the added benefit of testing your accuracy and coordination. (We all love a challenge, right?)

Where to Next

As before, apply this new sequence to the other chromatic patterns we've covered. (You should know these by now!) Want extra credit? Try playing each pattern without using a pick. Now that's graduating with honors!

7

Crossing Boundaries

This chapter provides a series of key workouts to get you moving around the fretboard and shifting smoothly between strings.

Overview

In the previous chapters, we've covered a lot of ground! We started with an intensive examination of right-hand technique before moving to key workouts for left-hand stamina, strength, and control. We then looked at a series of exercises for synchronizing both hands (and engaging that beautiful brain of yours!). Finally, tying many of these ideas together, we explored a rigorous set of legato drills for improved tone, dexterity, and playing speed.

If you've made it this far, well done. Treat yourself to something nice! If anyone asks, tell them you're celebrating a new level of musical enlightenment, forged by the rigors of achieving technical proficiency, in the pursuit of complete fretboard mastery—fueled by the spirit of all things rock 'n' roll! (Either that or just smile and shrug.)

In the final two chapters, we'll cover even more ground (quite literally, in terms of fretboard real estate). This chapter deals with the first challenge: *crossing boundaries*. In other words, moving fluently between strings in a variety of ways. To do this, we'll explore some important ideas for navigating the fretboard vertically across all six strings. Ready for a new level of coordination, dexterity, and speed? Let's go!

Stepping-Stones

This section explores some simple one-note-per-string sequences. The importance of this is twofold. First, these patterns provide an excellent left-hand workout for covering a lot of ground quickly. And second, they serve as a fantastic initiation into the world of *sweep* picking. (As mentioned in **Chapter 2**, this means playing multiple notes in one consecutive motion.) It's a technique responsible for many incomprehensibly fast licks that have baffled and delighted us since the dawn of rock!

Exercise 7.1

How to Do It

Loop across all six strings, playing one note per string on adjacent fingers. Starting on the 7th fret of the low E string, alternate between strings with your 1st and 2nd fingers, as illustrated below. Next, practice this drill with your 2nd and 3rd fingers (8th and 9th frets), followed by your 3rd and 4th fingers (9th and 10th frets).

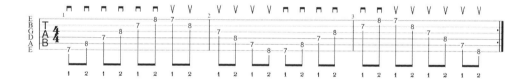

What to Focus On

- As always, start slowly, focusing on the accuracy and clarity of each note.
- Use palm muting to play notes cleanly and avoid strings ringing together.
- Remember, unlike alternate picking, here strokes move in the same direction.

Why It's Beneficial

This exercise is fantastic for engaging both hands. It requires left-hand control and coordination and is great for honing those sweep-picking chops!

Where to Next

Once comfortable, increase the fret spacing by shifting this exercise down toward the headstock (one fret at a time). Be sure to practice this with all adjacent finger combinations.

How to Do It

Now, let's try the previous exercise, this time using *non-adjacent* fingers. Starting on the low E string, alternate between the 7th and 9th frets with your 1st and 3rd fingers, as illustrated below. Next, practice these repetitions with your 2nd and 4th fingers, and 1st and 4th fingers in turn (using their respective frets).

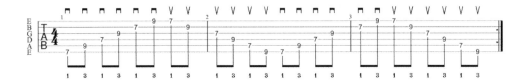

What to Focus On

- As always, keep your fingers close to the strings to avoid flapping about.
- Fret notes using your fingertips to maintain the natural curve of your fingers.
- Remember to hold your pick securely but not *tightly*—there's a big difference!

Why It's Beneficial

Another great exercise to get your fingers around. It's the same as the previous drill —just a smidgen harder. Enjoy!

Where to Next

Again, increase the stretches required in this exercise by gradually shifting down toward the headstock.

How to Do It

Finally, let's borrow from the previous chapter by throwing an alternate string sequence into the mix. Here we'll apply a *three-steps-forward, one-step-back* pattern, as shown below. Be sure to practice this with all finger variations outlined in the previous two exercises (both adjacent and non-adjacent). This example uses the 1st and 4th fingers:

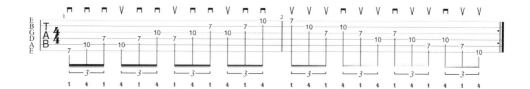

What to Focus On

- Monitor your finger pressure—remember, there's no need to push too hard!
- Don't rush things. (Playing badly at a fast tempo doesn't impress anybody.)
- Remember to stop periodically and check that your body remains relaxed.

Why It's Beneficial

This is an excellent way to get more mileage from one-note-per-string patterns—gotta love those string sequences!

Where to Next

Now, practice stretching incrementally all adjacent and non-adjacent finger combinations toward the headstock.

Rolling Stones

In the previous section, we covered some essentials for navigating the width of the fretboard. Here, we'll look at another key mechanism in transitioning across strings smoothly: *finger rolls*. This involves maneuvering between the tips and pads of your fingers. We can use this technique to alternate seamlessly between adjacent strings on the same fret. So…let's get rolling!

Exercise 7.4

How to Do It

For this first exercise, we'll begin with the finger-roll basics. Starting on the 7th fret, practice moving between the E and A strings using only your 1st finger. To do this, alternate between the tip and pad of your finger (without shifting from the 7th fret). When it feels comfortable, practice this technique with all four fingers, moving chromatically across each string as follows:

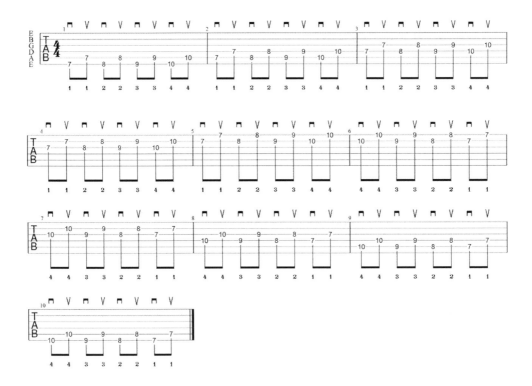

What to Focus On

- Finger rolls aren't *double-stops*. Each note should sound independently.
- Slightly lift off the string not being played to avoid notes ringing together.
- Once comfortable, this rolling motion should feel like one fluid movement.

Why It's Beneficial

Finger rolls take time to coordinate. (Particularly with that pesky pinky!) That said, it's a hugely beneficial technique to master. Beyond improving finger dexterity, it's used routinely across all spheres of rhythm and lead playing.

Where to Next

Remember all those chromatic sequences from **Chapter 5**? Given your newfound passion for finger rolls, it seems like a mighty fine time to experiment with these. Give it a go!

Exercise 7.5

How to Do It

Got the basics covered? Good. Now for a friendly bit of chaos! This time, instead of starting each roll on the lower string, every second and fourth note will alternate in the opposite direction. In other words, ascending through the chromatic sequence, your 2nd and 4th fingers will roll in reverse (from pads to fingertips). For example:

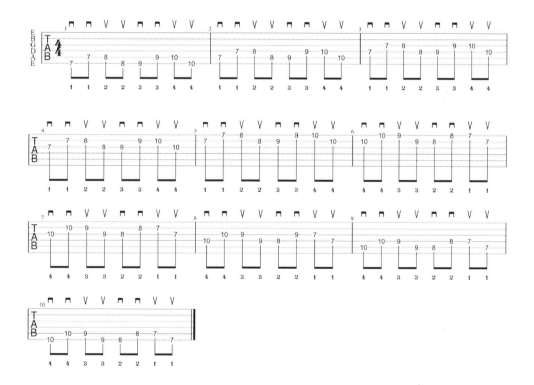

What to Focus On

- Again, each note should sound cleanly without ringing into the next.
- Refrain from palm muting to better assess the accuracy of your left hand.
- Spend time practicing your reverse rolls in isolation (using all four fingers).

Why It's Beneficial

This is another fantastic drill—especially for that pinky of yours! Again, it takes time to master, but when in doubt, *roll* with it. (Pun intended.)

Where to Next

Once comfortable with the basic ascending sequence, be sure to mix things up. As before, use this drill to experiment with the sequence variations from **Chapter 5**.

Exercise 7.6

How to Do It

Okay, time for the big mama of finger-roll workouts! For this exercise, beyond alternating the 2nd and 4th fingers in reverse, we'll also extend our finger rolls across *three* strings (yeah, you heard me!). To demonstrate, here's an example using triplets:

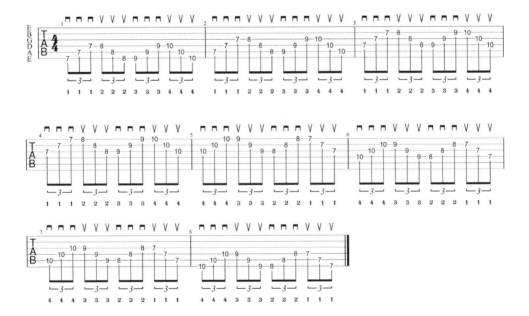

What to Focus On

- Practice your three-string finger rolls on each finger in isolation first.
- Again, avoid muting to better hone the execution of your finger rolls.
- You know the drill. Start slowly, playing notes with clarity and precision.

Why It's Beneficial

Extending across three strings will really test the dexterity of those digits! It also provides a great sweep-picking workout for the right hand. There's a treasure trove of technical goodness here.

Where to Next

Time to experiment with the sequence variations from **Chapter 5**. For a bonus, try switching the alternating finger sequence (rolling your 1st and 3rd fingers in reverse, instead of the 2nd and 4th). Have fun!

Sweeping Stones

In this final section, we'll end with a series of fantastic workouts for moving vertically across the fretboard. Executing these drills requires complete synchronicity between both hands. As such, we'll hark back to the essentials of great technique: coordination, control, and accuracy. (Sick of these terms yet? Good.) There's some absolute gold here—better bookmark this section now!

Exercise 7.7

How to Do It

Sticking with the theme of vertical movement, let's revisit the diagonal shapes from **Chapter 4**. Begin on the 7th fret of the low E string and sweep diagonally across the bottom four strings. Next, continue up and back, repeating this pattern from the A and D strings in sequence, as outlined:

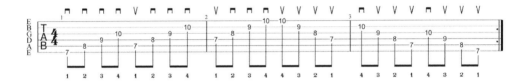

What to Focus On

- Make sure every note is separate and distinct—we're not playing chords.
- Remember to release each string after sounding a note to stop it ringing.
- Experiment with some right-hand dampening to further isolate your notes.

Why It's Beneficial

Learning to navigate one-note-per-string shapes is great for hand coordination, both in terms of individual precision and overall synchronization.

Where to Next

Instead of sweep picking, try using these diagonal patterns to test your *alternate* picking. I dare you!

How to Do It

Next, using the same concept, let's switch things up by inverting the diagonal shape of our fingers. This time, start at the 10th fret, again sweeping across each string in groups of four. Loop this exercise back and forth as outlined:

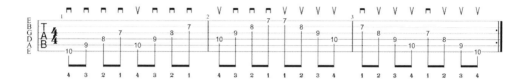

What to Focus On

- It's easy to rush. Don't! Focus on playing *well*, not playing quickly.
- Monitor your thumb position so it sits comfortably behind the neck.
- Keep your wrist straight to maintain the natural curve of your left hand.

Why It's Beneficial

This one complements the previous exercise well. Leading with your pinky finger is great for working the smallest and least endowed of your digits!

Where to Next

Again, use this exercise to practice your alternate picking. (Your technique will thank you later.)

How to Do It

This final variation is a mashup of the previous two. (Double the difficulty. Double the benefit. Double the fun. Right?) Sticking with our diagonal shapes, sweep across all six strings in groups of four. This time, however, let's ascend and descend by alternating between both shapes. We can demonstrate this as follows:

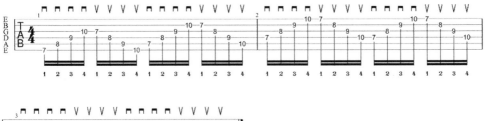

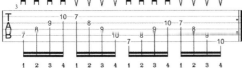

What to Focus On

- Concentrate on fretting each string accurately, using your fingertips.
- Remember, applying palm dampening will help isolate notes cleanly.
- Try to minimize excess movement by keeping fingers close to the strings.

Why It's Beneficial

Okay, I won't lie. This one's tough! That said, it's a great workout, and once you get it down, it doubles as a fantastic warm-up too. (One of my personal favorites.)

Where to Next

As before, practice this exercise using alternate picking. Looking for top marks? Try inverting each shape, starting from the 10th fret and leading with your pinky!

8

Breaking Boundaries

We've saved the best until last! This final chapter spans the fretboard with an onslaught of challenges to stretch the edges of your ability.

Overview

Well done. You've reached the home stretch! In the previous chapter, we looked at key workouts for moving vertically across the fretboard. As promised, this chapter continues our expedition into breaking boundaries. Here we'll pivot from the mechanics of crossing strings to the challenge of shifting horizontally on the guitar neck.

The focus for this chapter is finger coordination. Sounds easy considering all the hard work you've done, right? Well, there's one important caveat: We'll explore this while ascending and descending through various fretboard positions. No point in going easy just because we're near the finish line! (Consider this my parting gift. You're welcome.)

This chapter starts by outlining the usefulness of basic octave shapes. It then looks at a handful of key chord progressions before returning to the world of diagonal patterns. Ready to complete your journey? Well, prime those digits with some light stretching, grab that protein bar, stay hydrated, and let's rock 'n' roll!

Octave Frenzy

To kick off our horizontal workouts, this section centers around one key theme: *octaves*. Here we'll demonstrate how to transform some basic shapes into a glistening array of intense finger gymnastics. This one's for all you finger-coordination junkies out there!

How to Do It

Starting on the 3rd fret of the A string, sound this note, followed by its octave (5th fret, G string). Use this shape to ascend chromatically between the 3rd and 14th frets. Sound easy? Here's the catch: You must alternate between your 1st and 3rd and your 2nd and 4th fingers, as outlined. For some added spice, we'll also apply a *four-steps-forward, two-steps-back* sequence. To demonstrate:

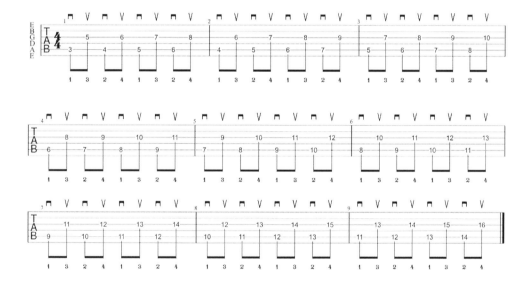

What to Focus On

- When switching shapes, focus on getting both fingers to land in unison.
- Practice keeping each shape planted for its full duration between beats.
- Be mindful to maintain good thumb position while ascending the neck.

Why It's Beneficial

As promised, this is a great exercise for coordinating multiple fingers while transitioning through various positions on the fretboard.

Where to Next

Now, try this exercise *descending* (starting with the shape on the 14th fret, heading to home base on the 3rd). This time, reverse the picking sequence to begin with the upper octaves on the G string. And don't forget to alternate those fingers!

Exerciso 8.2

How to Do It

Next, we'll use the same note sequence but change the octave shape. To do this, start with your 3rd finger on the 3rd fret of the A string. Play this note, followed by its octave (1st fret, B string). Using this pattern, ascend the fretboard, alternating between your 1st and 3rd and your 2nd and 4th fingers as follows:

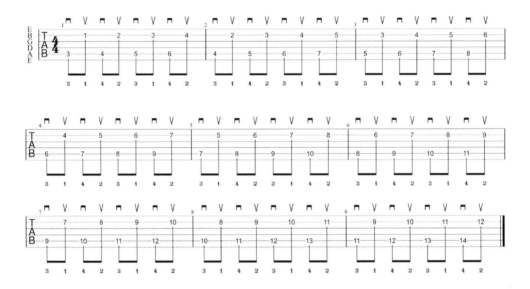

What to Focus On

- Again, when switching shapes, ensure that both fingers land at the same time.
- Use your thumb to help anchor your hand but avoid squeezing too hard.
- Focus on picking consistency in moving between the A and B strings.

Why It's Beneficial

Beyond the added difficulty in right-hand accuracy, this exercise also introduces a bigger stretch for those left-hand digits to navigate.

Where to Next

As before, practice descending this exercise in reverse. Don't forget to flip the picking sequence, starting with the upper octaves on the B string. (And again, remember to alternate fingers!)

Exercise 8.3

How to Do It

Ready for some octave insanity? You got it! This final exercise fuses the previous two. This time we'll practice moving between the 3rd and 14th frets, using *both* octave shapes. To do this, ascend through each shape, using both sets of fingers as shown:

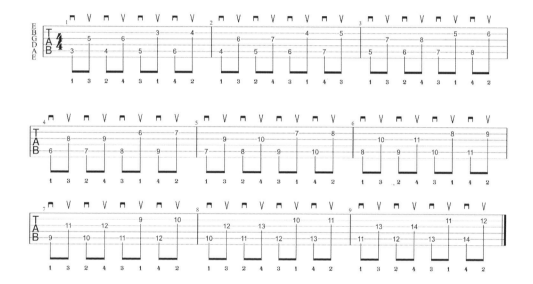

What to Focus On

- As before, it's important to coordinate your fingers to move in unison.
- Note that we're only switching shapes; the note sequence hasn't changed.
- As always, sound notes cleanly—sloppy practice begets sloppy playing.

Why It's Beneficial

Welcome to octaves unleashed, this section's crowning jewel! There are multiple challenges that make this exercise fantastic: finger coordination, picking accuracy, left-hand position, and so on. (Start slowly—I'm sure you'll nail it in no time.)

Where to Next

As with the previous drills, now try this exercise in reverse. Want a real test? Start at the 1st fret and ascend to the highest point possible on your fretboard (and then back again). Now that's a challenge!

Chord Frenzy

In the previous exercises, we transformed basic octave shapes into a horizontal workout blitz. That said, the next few drills really up the ante! In this section, we'll turn some simple chord shapes into a series of *not-so-simple* exercises. Looking for a challenge? These chord workouts are the ultimate in finger-twisting fun! Godspeed.

Exercise 8.4

How to Do It

This exercise revolves around two easy chord shapes. Simple, right? Well, don't get too excited! Things become a little more complicated when we put them together. Moving between the 3rd and 14th frets, ascend one fret at a time by alternating between the two chords outlined below:

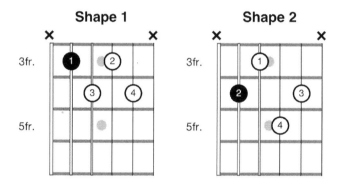

What to Focus On

- It's important that you follow the finger suggestions as outlined above.
- Focus on moving between shapes accurately, landing on your fingertips.
- Instead of strumming, pick notes individually to ensure they sustain clearly.

Why It's Beneficial

The beauty (or bane) of this exercise is that each finger moves to a new string between shapes. It's a short master class in left-hand accuracy and coordination. Good luck!

Where to Next

Now, start at the 14th fret and *descend* in the opposite direction. Don't forget to alternate chord shapes using the fingers outlined.

Exercise 8.5

How to Do It

Next, let's take the same idea but experiment with some fresh grips! Once again, move between the 3rd and 14th frets, ascending in half steps. This time, practice shifting between the two new shapes as outlined:

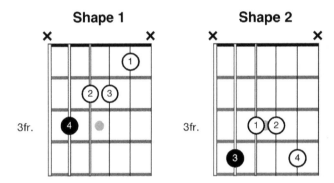

What to Focus On

- Again, ensure that you follow the finger suggestions as demonstrated above.
- Remember to test your accuracy by picking each note separately—no cheating!
- Monitor your thumb position, being careful not to grip the neck too tightly.

Why It's Beneficial

As before, in this exercise each finger must move to a new string between shapes. Yet another fantastic example of using chords to test those digits!

Where to Next

Once again, try descending this exercise in reverse, making sure to alternate shapes using the fingers outlined.

How to Do It

This final exercise is like the previous two but on steroids! For this drill, we'll combine our shapes to create a four-chord finger frenzy. (Try saying that 10x fast!) Moving between the 3rd and 14th frets, loop the progression, as illustrated below. To do this, ascend by beginning each cycle a half step higher than the last. (Note: Shape 3 and Shape 4 now start from the same fret.)

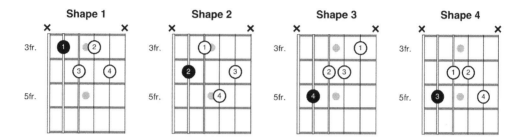

What to Focus On

- You know the drill: Use the fingers outlined and pick each note separately.
- Start slowly, landing each shape cleanly—no buzzing or fretting out, please!
- Remember, don't press too hard, and keep your hand as relaxed as possible.

Why It's Beneficial

A bevy of mind-bending, finger-twisting chaos. Enjoy!

Where to Next

Mastered the exercise? Great. Time to do it backward! Start at the 14th fret (with Shape 4) and loop the entire sequence in reverse.

Zig-Zag Frenzy

Well done on your quest for technical wizardry. You've reached the final section of this book! (And I've saved my favorites until last.) Here we'll build on the previous sections with some especially challenging embellishments. It's an almighty series of workouts to test your accuracy and hand synchronization. Perhaps it's best that you approach this section with a pinch of fear and trepidation.

Exercise 8.7

How to Do It

In this first exercise, we'll revisit the diagonal shapes from **Chapter 4** and merge them with the chordal movements from the previous section. The result: A killer workout bound to get those fingers primed! To do this, ascend one fret at a time, alternating between the two shapes outlined below. This time, start at the 1st fret and continue to the highest point you can reach on the fretboard.

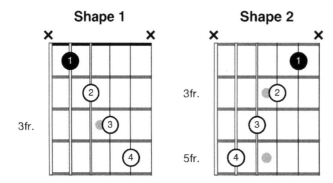

What to Focus On

- Remember to shift up one half step with every chord change.
- Make sure you sound notes individually to check for accuracy.
- Focus on landing your fingertips in the upper half of each fret.

Why It's Beneficial

This exercise is tough. It shifts positions rapidly and requires a great deal of finger coordination. Better get practicing!

Where to Next

Once comfortable, start at the highest point possible on your fretboard and try *descending* in reverse. (Note: The number and accessibility of your frets depends on the type of guitar.)

Exercise 8.8

How to Do It

This exercise builds on the previous one. Using our diagonal shapes, start at the 1st fret and move to the highest point possible on your fretboard. (For example, on my guitar it's the 20th fret.) However, this time we'll introduce one big tweak. Instead of playing each shape as a chord, let's turn them into sweep-picking patterns! Here's an example:

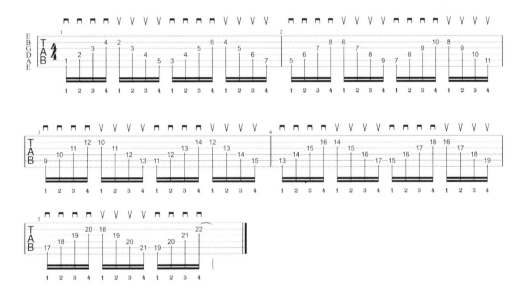

What to Focus On

- Remember, we're no longer playing chords. Sound each note in isolation.
- Focus on your timing, coordinating both hands together with precision.
- Minimize your hand movements to stay close to the strings at all times.

Why It's Beneficial

Another killer workout for accuracy and hand synchronization. And did I mention it's one of my favorites?

Where to Next

Time to rewind. Starting from the highest position you can reach, be sure to put those masterful descending skills of yours into practice. (Don't worry if you struggle playing the top few frets, just use the highest point your reach allows.)

Exercise 8.9

How to Do It

Okay, ready for something extreme? (It seems fitting to end with a bang.) For this final variation, let's take the previous exercise, throw string skipping into the mix, and see what happens! As before, begin at the 1st fret and ascend to the highest point you can reach. This time, however, we'll use alternate strokes to skip between the 1st and 3rd and then 2nd and 4th fingers as outlined:

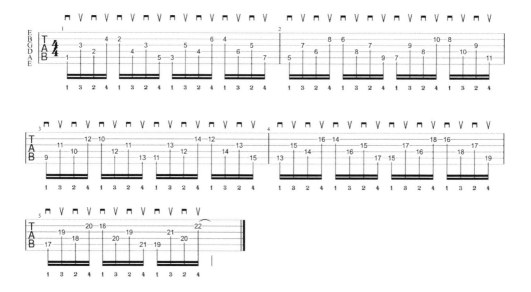

What to Focus On

- Start slowly, concentrating on picking accuracy and hand synchronization.
- Use your 1st finger to provide a visual anchor point when ascending.
- Pay attention to that pinky finger—it's the cheeky, rebellious sort!

Why It's Beneficial

Yep, there's no free ride. The more you put in, the more you get out—it's how things work! (By the way, this exercise reminds me of how a robot might sound when calculating something. A pointless insight, sure...but I just wanted to lighten the mood.)

Where to Next

Now, see if you can do it in reverse. Looking for a little extra stimulation? How about inverting each shape to lead with your 4th finger? Go ahead, try it!

Final Thoughts

Congratulations on completing **Total Guitar Workout**!

You've made it through the labyrinth of tests, hurdles, and challenges. Through this expedition, we discovered the keys to right-hand accuracy and ventured into the mechanics of left-hand control. We explored the depths of hand synchronization and traversed the entire fretboard in search of speed and dexterity. All this while building strength, coordination, stamina, and grit (the most valuable skill of all!).

Yep, this book was comprehensive! Nonetheless, the goal wasn't to cover every approach in building good technique. That would be needlessly overwhelming, not to mention impossible. Instead, much thought went into what to include, and by implication what *not* to include. Here we've concentrated on the most important elements for the greatest impact. The purpose was to provide clear direction while empowering your own experimentation and discovery.

Beyond learning practice drills, this book is a platform for adapting and developing your own exercises. As such, it will hopefully serve as an ongoing reference tool. The more familiar you are with these workouts, the more you can customize them to suit you. After all, that's the challenge of learning anything worthwhile—applying it to your unique situation. Information remains dormant until manifest in action. (That's some ancient wisdom right there!)

Finally, let's conclude in the spirit with which we opened: *Effective practice requires a healthy balance*. While warm-ups and workouts are foundational, *foundations* exist for building on. Great technique isn't an end in itself; its purpose is to serve musicality. And here lies the paradox—the point of it all. We must never let our desire to improve at playing music distract us from the enjoyment of actually *playing music*!

May this book help inspire you toward continued learning and creativity.

Liked This Book?

Did you find this book useful? You can make a big difference in helping us spread the word!

While it would be nice to have the promotional muscle of a major publishing house, independent authors rely heavily on the loyalty of their audience. Online reviews are one of the most powerful tools we have for getting attention and finding new readers.

If you found this book helpful, please consider helping us by leaving an online review at your place of purchase. Reviews needn't be long or in-depth; a star rating with a short comment is perfect. If you could take a minute to leave your feedback, it would be sincerely appreciated!

Additional Resources

For more resources, including great free content, be sure to visit us at:

www.guitariq.com

Stay in touch with all the latest news. To connect with us online, head to:

www.guitariq.com/connect

Would you like to read more? For a complete list of Luke's books, check out:

www.guitariq.com/books

Remember to grab your online bonus! Get the free bonus content for this book at:

www.guitariq.com/tgw-bonus

Interested in a master class with Luke? To check out his online workshops, go to:

www.guitariq.com/academy

About the Author

Having played for over 25 years, Luke Zecchin is an accomplished guitarist with a wealth of studio and live experience. Outside his work teaching music, Luke has toured extensively alongside renowned national and international acts, performing at everything from clubs, theaters, and festivals to various appearances on commercial radio and national television.

Playing lead guitar, Luke has worked on projects with established international producers and engineers. He has been fortunate to see these collaborations break into both the Top 50 ARIA Album and Singles charts, having also received nationwide airplay and notable debuts on the Australian iTunes Rock charts.

As the founder of **GuitarIQ.com**, Luke is dedicated to the education and coaching of guitar players all over the globe. With books available in over 100 countries worldwide, he has emerged as an international chart-topping author in his field.

Luke continues to work as an author and musician from his project studio based in the Adelaide Hills, South Australia.

Find him online at **LukeZecchin.com**.

Printed in Great Britain
by Amazon

86030295R00068